STAR TREK

THE MOVIES

TITAN

WWW.TITAN-COMICS.COM

Star Trek
The Movies – Volume One
ISBN: 978178585924

Published by Titan
A division of Titan Publishing
Group Ltd.,
144 Southwark Street,
London
SE1 0UP

Collecting the best articles and
interviews from *Star Trek* Magazine.

A CIP catalogue record for this title
is available from the British Library.

First Edition June 2016
10 9 8 7 6 5 4 3 2 1

Printed in China.

Editor Christopher Cooper
Senior Editor Martin Eden
Art Director Oz Browne
Studio Manager Emma Smith
Publishing Manager Darryl Tothill
Publishing Director Chris Teather
Operations Director Leigh Baulch
Executive Director Vivian Cheung
Publisher Nick Landau

Acknowledgments:
Titan Would Like to Thank...
The casts and crews of *Star Trek*,
J.J. Abrams and Bad Robot,
Paramount Pictures, and John
Van Citters and Marian Cordry at
CBS Consumer Products for their
invaluable assistance in putting this
volume together.

CONTENTS

MAKING *STAR TREK*

INTERVIEWS

FEATURES

SPACE, THE FINAL FRONTIER...

For 50 Earth years, *Star Trek* has grown from a popular, yet ultimately short-lived NBC television series, into a global, multi-media sensation – and credit for that transformation can be attributed, in no small part, to its success on the silver screen.

The original *Star Trek* cast reunited for a hit run of six classic movies, with *The Next Generation* taking up the mantle for a further four 24th Century outings. In 2009, *Star Trek* would come full circle, albeit in an alternate universe, with J.J. Abrams in the director's chair. A new generation of fans would thrill to the early adventures of a younger Jim Kirk, just beginning his mission of exploration and discovery.

As *Star Trek Beyond* opens a new chapter in Gene Roddenberry's futuristic saga, this special edition collects the best material from *The Official Star Trek Magazine*, for an in-depth look at the movies which took the franchise to another dimension.

Christopher Cooper – Editor, *Star Trek Magazine*

J.J. ABRAMS

DIRECTING
STAR TREK INTO DARKNESS

Described by Benedict Cumberbatch as a polymath, J.J. Abrams approaches every project with absolute dedication, gusto, and more than a touch of creative genius. Before embarking on his wildly successful adventure in a galaxy far, far, away, the director revealed his passion for *Star Trek* isn't something he's going to let go anytime soon.
Interview by Tara Bennett

J.J. Abrams with writer Alex Kurtzman

I f you haven't figured it out by now, don't bet against J.J. Abrams. As a writer, producer, director (and even composer), Abrams has been figuring out how to tell stories in the most engaging and surprising way possible since he was a little kid, making Super 8 films with his buddies. Once he graduated from college, he threw himself into the business, and made his

mark as the guy that created TV shows like *Lost*, *Fringe* and *Alias* – high-concept shows that looked like an impossible sell to the mainstream viewing public, yet became modern era water-cooler classics.

Success on the small screen opened the door to movies, where he's helped reinvigorate a myriad of genres from found-footage films

"WE KNEW THERE HAD TO BE A MORE COMPLEX STORY, A DEEPER STORY, BECAUSE THE FIRST FILM WAS SORT OF GLORIOUSLY INNOCENT."

Chekov in action

(*Cloverfield*) to blockbuster action films (*Mission: Impossible III*), and even bygone Spielbergian kid adventure films (*Super 8*). So when Abrams and his Bad Robot creative team signed on to make *Star Trek* relevant to a new generation, in 2009, no one should have second-guessed him because, well, we know how things turned out.

Back in May 2013, audiences were beside themselves with excitement for its sequel, *Star Trek Into Darkness*, awaiting the continuing adventures of Captain James Kirk (Chris Pine), Mr. Spock (Zachary Quinto) and their crew of rebooted, yet equally beloved characters. Abrams' big gamble in 2009 hit the jackpot with a new generation of moviegoers, long-time *Trek* fans, and critics alike. But as everyone knows, in Hollywood it's not enough to get it right and go away. The real test is repeating the magic... and that's where things get really scary.

Luckily, Abrams isn't afraid of a challenge, and the director admits that while he and his

> "THE IDEA OF AN ACTION SEQUENCE THAT IS HARROWING, EXCITING, AND SCARY, INVOLVING KLINGONS AND OUR CHARACTERS, WAS TOO DELICIOUS TO PASS UP."

team may not be the underdogs anymore, it was *Star Trek* itself that was their creative ace-in-the-hole. Abrams explains, "I feel like when the first *Star Trek* we did came out there hadn't really been movies in a while, and people were down on *Star Trek*. In a way, we came into it as a great situation, in that we could really reinvent

it. Now we are coming into it on the heels of what we did last time. You never really know why some things work. It is alchemy, and you can't really prepare and know exactly how it's going to work because there's magic in how it functions. So following in our own example, you hope and pray, and work your ass off to achieve a similar magic. I think the key to that are the characters that [Gene] Roddenberry created that we've tried to bring back, and do them and do him proud. And then part of it is that the actors are extraordinary in the roles. Part of it is the incredible editors, designers, composer, the costume designer... everyone, with very few exceptions, came back [for the sequel], and I think we all felt we have to outdo ourselves not with scale, or bombast, or pyrotechnics, but to maintain the thing we did last time. Despite it being called *Star Trek*, it had to be real. You had to feel it. Yes, it's hyper real, and a little bit more of a bigger show than life with a future view of humanity, but at the core it only works because you desperately love these characters."

TESTING TIMES

Since the first film came out, fans and entertainment outlets have been relentlessly suggesting and speculating about where the sequel could go. Couple all of that chatter with 40-plus years of actual *Trek* canon to consider, and you could easily become fetal in the corner with indecision. Abrams says he and his writing team of Bob Orci, Alex Kurtzman, Damon Lindelof, and Bryan Burk bypassed that by leaning on their trusted internal instincts. "I think certainly Bob, Damon and Alex are in tune with what the fans are saying and what they want. While I am as well, I feel like those

Star Trek Into Darkness director J.J. Abrams

guys are more wired, or wireless, than I am. I feel like anecdotally I hear what certain people are saying. I came to this [franchise] as more of an outsider. I entered this world really intrigued by it, but not really a pre-existing fan. However, Bob is obsessed," he laughs. "I feel like the great thing about that was that we were able to be aware of the chatter, just like in the first movie, hearing what people might want, or not want, or expect or resent, or have to be concerned about. At the same time, Bryan (who had never seen an episode) and I were able to approach this with a spectrum of points of view. While people were [suggesting] things, none of that really mattered much to me, because I felt I was coming from the point of the moviegoer who just wants to be entertained, understand, and care about the world and the characters. I will say nothing matters more to us than the fans, and making sure they are getting something they love. But having said that, we can't make a movie for pre-existing *Star Trek* fans, we have to make a movie for moviegoers, and if you happen to be a *Star Trek* fan, you'll benefit because we are looking out for you, and we respect what you are bringing to the film. The goal here is to cast a wide net and get people into the theater that might think *Star Trek* sucks, and then they realize they had a rousing time and cared desperately about these characters, like *Trek* fans have for years."

Abrams says they knew creatively they wanted *Star Trek Into Darkness* to test the still green Captain Kirk and his adjusting crew not long after the events of the original film. "We knew there had to be a more complex story, a deeper story, because the first film was sort of gloriously innocent in all these people coming together that didn't know each other. So the second film is really about testing those relationships by default, in that they have to go through something more extreme and more intense. While Kirk went through a hell of an adventure, and found a family, I think he also was put in to the position of Captain prematurely. What this movie does is prove that, and force him and the rest of the crew to step up. The question is will they, and can they survive?"

ANOTHER DIMENSION

Kirk and company's journey will get played out on an epic scale, because Abrams admits that his *Trek* films also have to function as massive event movies, utilizing all of the best technology and movie-making wizardry that a sci-fi space film demands. In trying to raise the creative bar, Abrams admits that *Star Trek Into Darkness* has

Uhura: back on the Bridge

turned out to be his most challenging directorial effort by far. "I think part of it was the scope of it," he explains. "The scale of the movie was pretty huge. I think that it was also about trying to take what we did before and embrace the things that worked, and try some things that we hadn't done. Part of it was realizing there are always things [in the original] that I look at and wish I had done this or that. It's a little bit of a second chance to try and do some things that didn't quite work the way I wanted them to, and then do some things I didn't get a chance to do before."

From a technological standpoint, Abrams upped the ante by shooting several sequences in IMAX, and by also committing to doing a 3D print (achieved through a new 2D to 3D conversion process) for the first time. "Shooting IMAX is a hassle," he laughs frankly about the inherent issues with those decisions. "The cameras are huge, heavy, and loud. But for all the obvious problems, it is worth every difficulty and delay

you have, because the quality of the image is extraordinary. As for the 3D thing, I never had a huge issue with it, but I was never actively a fan. When I started to see some of the images from the first film converted into 3D, I was amazed how well the 3D conversion works. It used to be something correctly assumed to be a lesser approach, and the quality suffers for it. We are doing some new techniques that I think push the experience, while allowing people like myself, who never really enjoyed [3D], and in some cases couldn't even see it – there were times I felt like my eyes crossed – to get it. This new process uses multiple virtual cameras to push the perspective and depth in certain ways, toward how people see in 3D. It mitigates the problems that cause people like me not to get it. Ultimately I feel like, looking at what we have, there are moments that truly make me laugh because we go from hopefully cool compositions in 2D to something that is more of a rollercoaster ride in

J.J. Abrams with Bob Orci on set

Quinto and Pine as Spock and Kirk

J.J. Abrams takes the *Enterprise* crew *Into Darkness*

3D. And that's not to say the 2D experience wasn't the primary focus. All I wanted to do was make sure I made a movie that was working in 2D, but if you see it in 3D you get a little more bang for your buck."

Going back to story, Abrams says they throw a few adversaries at Kirk to really push the action in this film. He teases that old school *Trek* fans will finally get to savor the introduction of Klingons. "It's an important story point, as you'll see in the movie. While the idea of Klingons was something we wanted to do in the first movie, they ended up being superfluous, given the story of Nero (Eric Bana). It complicated his back story a little bit, and now there's a real logic to why we bring them into this film. Plus we couldn't do two movies and not have the Klingons," he chuckles. "The idea of an action sequence that is harrowing, exciting, and scary, involving Klingons and our characters, was too delicious to pass up."

THROWING DOWN THE GAUNTLET

Abrams also touches on Benedict Cumberbatch's John Harrison, who will have a very deep story

> "MY INVOLVEMENT IN THE NEXT FILM IS WITHOUT QUESTION. I LOVE THIS WHOLE UNIVERSE, AND THESE PEOPLE, TOO MUCH."

that will work for new fans and old fans. "Nero was a wonderfully worthy adversary for a newly-forged team, but [here] we needed someone who would get under their skin, and challenge them in a way they could have never survived when they first came together. We always knew it was going to be more of an extreme story, pushing limits dramatically and emotionally. There would be more questions of who to trust, and of manipulation and difficulty, rather than just a raving, lunatic Romulan. We were going to have someone who could push the buttons of the crew, and test the mettle of their relationships. So we always knew we would go darker, deeper, and really see what it's like for

these people to experience that, and can they get through that gauntlet alive."

The director says that Cumberbatch rises to the challenge of being all that and more in the film. "Damon suggested I watch *Sherlock*, which I had not seen. And like everyone who has seen it, I was gripped by his brilliance, his speeches, his sense of humor, and his voice is unparalleled. You cannot deny that he brings a crazy power to whatever he does. And ultimately, because of the story of Benedict's character, Kirk ends up being challenged in a way that is very specific to his story. I think it ends up being something that does push Kirk to a place he's never been before."

Of course, fans already want to know if there will be a *Trek* 3, and if the films were conceptualized to tell a story in three parts. Abrams says, "We've discussed a lot of possibilities about what might happen down the line. I wouldn't say there has been a trilogy planned. I would say there are a number of storylines that get us excited. We really are taking this journey one step at a time, and while there are a lot of ideas we have now for what might be a third movie, it's really up to the audience to determine if that is something that comes to pass."

However, the big question is: will Abrams be able to helm the next installment, considering his job as the director of the new *Star Wars* film? Abrams chuckles, "In the category of one step at a time, we're finishing this movie. I would say I have put too much of myself – we all have – into this world and these characters, that my involvement in the next film is without question. I love this whole universe, and these people, too much. If I end up directing another movie, that remains to be seen. We'll finish this one first then we can talk about the next one, if we get so lucky." ▲

J.J. Abrams and composer Michael Giacchino

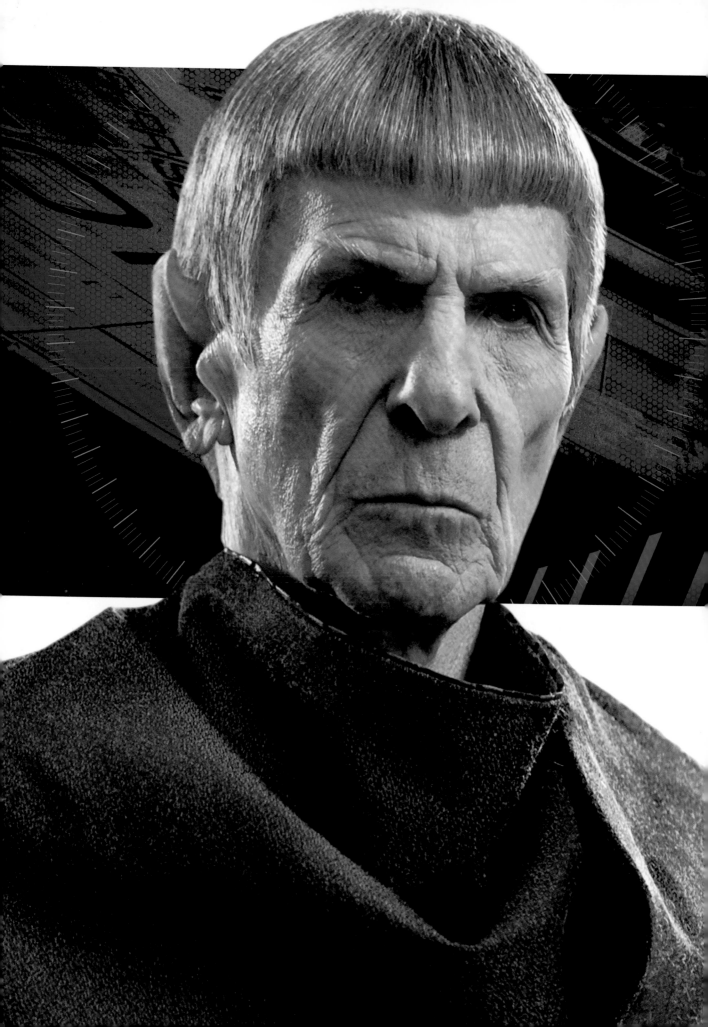

LEONARD NIMOY IS SPOCK PRIME

Leonard Nimoy, who passed away in early 2015, always said that he wouldn't return to playing Spock of Vulcan if the character was marginalized, so it was a pleasant surprise to be asked to be part of the new *Star Trek* film, in which not just the character of Spock, but his particular interpretation of it, is so central. Describing his return as "like stepping back into a well worn suit," Nimoy's involvement was a highpoint for fans and actors alike...

Leonard Nimoy sounds almost surprised when he's chatting about his return as Spock in the new feature film. "I had a grand time," he says. "I found myself thoroughly enjoying it. I was very comfortable, and I don't know how to account for it. I felt like a grandfather with a bunch of intelligent, evolving grandchildren, watching them at work, and enjoying working with them. I just felt very good about it – I felt totally at home doing it."

It's fair to say that Nimoy never seriously expected to be donning Spock's ears again – after all, his last appearance in the role was in a 1991 episode of *Star Trek: The Next Generation*. But the combination of the enthusiasm of producers J.J. Abrams, Roberto Orci and Alex Kurtzman and the story that they proposed to tell in their big-screen reinvention of the classic series, which had been part of Nimoy's life since 1964, meant that he signed on to pass the torch between the original incarnation of the characters and their successors.

The gap since fans last saw Spock is reflected within the fiction of the story as well. Nimoy doesn't see Spock as being on a direct line from the character he played in *TNG*'s "Unification." "My connection with the character is more in keeping with the personal development of the character, rather than the career development of the character," he explains. "My sense is that the last time we saw Spock, he was deep in the Romulan Empire on an ambassadorial mission.

In this movie, there's no direct connection to that, but I have a very strong feeling about the emotional line and that personal development of the character, which I'm most comfortable discussing.

"The most fascinating thing for me about working on this movie was not only to see all these young actors who are portraying the original *Star Trek* series characters, and watch them work extremely well, but also to work with them myself as Spock from another time plane. I see them, and have a wider view of who they are and where they're going. I know more about them in a way than they know about themselves. There's a kind of omniscience about the character."

The most interesting change for Nimoy is that "I think I found a certain peace with the character. The character I play as Spock in this movie is a character who is at peace with himself, whereas the Spock that Zachary Quinto has to play is in a condition that is prior to what we saw in the original series, and not quite as evolved as he was in the original series. He's in the process of finding himself. He's putting together the building blocks of his character that will arrive at the character that I portrayed in the original series. During the course of this particular movie, he finds a peace as Spock, and grows into the Spock that I portrayed in the original series."

Nimoy and Quinto spent quite a bit of time working together before shooting began on the movie.

"I found him to be very curious, very inquisitive, very intelligent," Nimoy praises. "He's a very talented actor. We had a very good time. We found each other and we were on a common page very quickly."

Talking to *Star Trek Magazine* in 2008, Nimoy teased that Quinto had found facets of Spock's character that simply hadn't occurred to him until he saw the younger actor in action. "It struck me at the end of the scene where Spock is having his meeting with the members of the Vulcan Academy," Nimoy now explains. "They are determining that he should be admitted to the Academy in spite of the fact that he's not a pure Vulcan. They're making an exception in his case, and making an allowance. He rejects the invitation, and the way that he rejects it I felt was extremely fresh and daring. It had an edge to it that surprised me – something that I would not have thought of as a choice.

"I WAS AWESTRUCK BY EVERYONE'S PROFESSIONALISM AND DEDICATION, AND THE UNDERSTANDING OF THE VALUES OF *STAR TREK*."

"I thought it was a wonderful choice on Zachary's part, and it told me very specifically, as I referred to earlier, that the Spock in that moment is not yet the Spock that I played in the series. He's before that Spock: he still has something in his being that makes him respond to stimuli differently than I would have playing the character that I was in the series.

"The way he told these people, and the subtext of what he was doing was a wonderful choice. He was telling them what he thought of them, and he did it in a way that was elegant and dramatic. I was kind of startled, frankly, by the way he said, 'Live long and

Spock on Delta Vega

Spock meets Spock

prosper!' It was quite wonderful. Zachary is very good. I wouldn't underestimate him for a moment. He's full of interesting ideas, intelligence and surprises. I think he could have a great career as Spock: if he wants it, it's there for him.

"I wouldn't be a bit surprised if there was more of that to come, and I sincerely hope so. I'm very proud to have been part of what has gone before, and I'm very glad to hand it off to such a talented person, and such talented people in general. All the people on the film were great fun to be with and to work with. To watch them on screen is a delight, as it was to see it all come together. There will be examinations, minutiae discussed about the differences between the original characters and these characters, the time frame, and the canon, and whether the canon has been dealt with properly, or whether it has been abused... but finally, I think this is a wonderfully entertaining and very human film. It's a very large film in its scope, but terribly human. I think the coming together of the characters is brilliantly handled."

"My mind to your mind..."

ADDING TO THE LORE

Nimoy laughs as he recalls watching Kirk finally getting on board his Starship. "The way in which McCoy contrives to get Kirk onto the Enterprise, in spite of the problems that Kirk was presented with – or rather, that Kirk is creating for himself – is just wonderful. The two of them work so well together: they were just so wonderful to watch."

Other moments in the film Nimoy particularly enjoyed include "My first meeting with Kirk in the film. It's a treat the way we find each other, and the way we work together from that moment on. The first scene with Simon Pegg as Scotty is a treat too. My final scene with Zachary Quinto is really quite remarkable, with the two Spocks coming face to face with each other."

That final scene sees Spock left in the 23rd Century, as his younger self and his old friends start to forge their futures. "I think it's interesting that Spock quickly comes to understand what is going on here," Nimoy says. "These young people are in the process of finding each other, and he has information that is helpful to accomplish that, to bring them to each other, and bring them into their proper relationship with each other. I think that is essentially Spock's function in this movie, and it's extremely well-written."

The new 23rd Century is very different from the one Spock lived through originally. Vulcan is gone, and Spock's mother Amanda with it. "It's very daring," Nimoy notes. "I think it's powerful, and it has its emotional impact on Spock, which it's supposed to do. It gives us a whole other

level of experience for these characters and their relationships, and for the story in general. I think they've added a tremendous amount of interesting lore to the franchise and the *Star Trek* story."

Although he got to spend time with Quinto, Nimoy's path didn't cross with Ben Cross, playing Spock's father Sarek, until quite late in the shoot. "I met him briefly when he was almost finished with the job," he recalls. "It was in the makeup department. We had a nice conversation but I think it was his last day of work. We had a brief conversation about careers and where he was living.

"I saw the scenes that he played in the movie, particularly the scene with the young Spock where he says he's going to have to determine how he lives his life. I saw the scene between him and Amanda, Winona

LEONARD NIMOY

Leonard Simon Nimoy was born in 1931 and carved out a career as an actor, film director, poet, musician and photographer. Raised by his immigrant parents in Boston, Nimoy began acting at age eight, gaining notice as a teen. He attended UCLA to study photography but left before obtaining his degree, which he finally obtained at Boston College. He also has a masters degree in education. After serving in the U.S. Army Reserve, Nimoy spent the 1950s and 1960s working on small budget films and numerous television series prior to landing the role of Spock on *Star Trek*. After earning three Emmy nominations for his work, he smoothly segued from *Star Trek* to *Mission: Impossible* for two seasons. In 1982, Nimoy earned a fourth Emmy nomination for the telefilm *A Woman Called Golda*.

While he continued to appear in film and television roles, he regularly returned to portray Spock, first in animation and then the feature film series. The latter led to the beginning of his career as a feature director with *Star Trek III: The Search for Spock* and *Star Trek IV: The Voyage Home* to his credit. His distinctive voice has been heard on numerous animated programs and video games including *Civilization IV*. On stage, he earned acclaim for his work in *Equus* and the one-man show *Vincent*, which he wrote. As an author, he has penned two autobiographies, volumes of poetry, and created the comic book series *Primortals*. Nimoy has also released five albums of music and song.

Recommended performance:
Morris Meyerson: A Woman Named Golda

Ryder. I thought they were wonderful: so touching, so personal. The chemistry amongst those people – Ben Cross, the young Spock and Amanda – was wonderful: they were vivid relationships."

Nimoy thought the casting of Ben Cross as a replacement for the original Sarek, Mark Lenard, was "a good choice. I had a wonderful time with Mark. He had such dignity and such elegance and grace. I admired him a lot, I admired the work he did. I always enjoyed working with him. I enjoyed directing him – he was very elegant and interesting, and such a good actor. We had our share of good times."

In the two weeks' shooting Nimoy did for the movie, scattered throughout the five month filming schedule, the director of *Star Trek III: The Search for Spock* and *Star Trek IV: The Voyage Home* realized that "this film is technically on a scale that I would not be able to handle. The technology has increased and evolved so far beyond the kind of thing that we were doing when I was making those films. It's beyond me. It takes a certain skill and an understanding of the technology that I do not have to achieve the integration of the sets with the extraordinary special effects that are in this film."

Nimoy laughs heartily at a description of J.J. Abrams juggling 3000 things in the air at once. "That's about the size of it, exactly. He's quite a remarkable director, he really is, and a marvelous person. I thoroughly enjoyed working for him.

"I was awestruck by everyone's professionalism and dedication, and the understanding of the values of *Star Trek*. It's just absolutely charming to watch these characters, to see their appreciation of each other and their professionalism, as in spite of their foibles, in spite of their differences, they come together as a team, in the way that this film brings them together."

Old friends meet for the first time

"THE CHARACTER I PLAY AS SPOCK IN THIS MOVIE IS A CHARACTER WHO IS AT PEACE WITH HIMSELF."

And should the sequel require some input from the older generation, Nimoy would be very happy to reprise the older Spock. "Of course, of course," he says enthusiastically. "If the phone rings again, and it's J.J. calling to talk about another project, I'm more than willing to enter a discussion about it, and explore it with him. I have the feeling that my involvement has run its course – but then again, I've had that feeling many times before. I've felt that I was finished with all this, so this was a very pleasant surprise to be called back after all these years and be able to make a contribution here. If it happens again, I would gladly work for him again.

"There are very few projects that could entice me now: I enjoy the photography that I do. It's a big part of my life, and I have a great deal of pleasure doing it, but if J.J. were to call again, I would certainly pay attention." ▲

Leonard Nimoy reprises the role of Spock

ROBERTO ORCI &
ALEX KURTZMAN
WRITERS / PRODUCERS

After two years of guarded conversations about the script for the new *Star Trek* reboot, writers and producers Roberto Orci and Alex Kurtzman finally have the chance to discuss the genesis of their story and the changes they made to the *Star Trek* universe...

Where did you come up with the idea of making this film a genesis story for the original crew, or was that a no-brainer as far as you were concerned?

Alex Kurtzman: When we were first asked in the broadest sense if we would ever consider doing *Star Trek*, it was like someone had just punched us in the solar plexus – just the idea that we would be able to inherit something like that. Before we even had any specific conversations, the idea of joining the legacy was so intense – and frightening, frankly, because it meant so much to us as kids. The fear of messing it up was the first feeling that we had. But talking about it, that's when we realized that's exactly why we had to do it. When something is that important to you, you have to protect it.

The immediate answer for all of us was that the only way we were interested in this was to do Kirk and Spock, going back to the genesis of the ship. We weren't interested in *The Next Generation*. This is where we wanted to live in it.

But we faced an immediate problem: we knew the fate of all the characters.

> ## "ONE OF THE FIRST IDEAS WE HAD WAS THAT LEONARD NIMOY HAD TO SOMEHOW BE THE CATALYST FOR OUR STORY. EVERYTHING STEMMED FROM THAT IDEA FOR US."

Roberto Orci: It occurred to us very early on that the show began on the five-year mission, and we realized that we hadn't actually seen all these characters meet and go on their first adventure. That became an obvious place to explore because the goal was to make sure that we had a *Star Trek* that made new audiences learn why fans like *Star Trek*. It couldn't rely on a previous knowledge of *Star Trek*. The fact that the origin story had not been covered, and that's what you'd naturally want to do to get new fans, just made it seem like a perfect thing to do.

Was that choice influenced by the success of *Batman Begins* and *Casino Royale* which were doing similar things with other franchises, or was it parallel evolution of ideas?

AK: I have to say that I don't think it was a conscious influence for us at all.

RO: It'll sound ridiculous I suppose, but for us as fans, it's both a prequel and a sequel. Through Leonard Nimoy's involvement, and the continuing story of Mr. Spock, if you're a fan it's a sequel – so there's no comparison with those other films.

Did you always intend to have Spock Prime's involvement?
RO: Always.
AK: We knew there was just no way to tell the story without Spock and everything he has represented in the show – and everything that Leonard Nimoy represents to us. He had to be the steward, not only to calibrate

our involvement and our compass to show we were pointing in the right direction, but also to show fans that Mr. Spock was blessing this divergent timeline and this story.

RO: It wasn't until we hit upon that idea that we thought we really knew how to do this. It was going to allow us to go back, but also allow us to make the changes we needed to make, and do it within the rules of *Star Trek*, and do it with the ambassador of *Star Trek* himself.

Did you ever worry you'd confuse audiences with the shifting timeline?
AK: Sure, of course. We were worried about it because any time travel story is either potentially the most emotionally rewarding – i.e. *Back to the Future* – or the most confusing, convoluted and least interesting.
RO: When you see the movie, we don't play with the time travel story in the traditional way. It's not "bumping into your parents and threatening your existence." It's used in a very subtle way – it's not even something you necessarily know is happening very early on.

The roadshow material carefully avoided the time travel aspect so it will have come as a surprise to audiences. Did you consciously decide to keep it hidden?
AK: Yes, because you don't want to say "It's a sequel and a prequel." People would be going, "What?"
RO: You want it to be clean, even if ultimately that is what it is.

Star Trek has numerous different philosophies of time travel – this appears to have a determinist philosophy. Was there a lot of discussion about that, or did you decide that was the trope you needed to get the pieces where you wanted them on the chess board?
AK: We talked very much about how we were going to use time travel. It's very much a magic bullet. It's something that has been used within continuity. The idea of changing history and going into parallel universes has been done in *Star Trek*, so it's a canon solution.

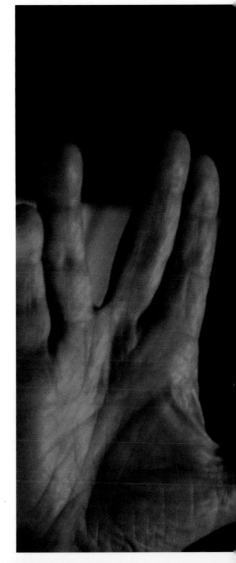

Spock (Leonard Nimoy) and Kirk (Chris Pine)

Did you ever consider a complete reboot?
RO: No, not for a second. That's why one of the first ideas we had was that Leonard Nimoy had to somehow be the catalyst for our story. Everything stemmed from that idea for us.
AK: It's funny you ask about time travel and the idea that time sorts itself out. There was a line that we had written that was shot which ended up getting cut from the movie. Watching it the other day, I wish we'd kept

it. When Kirk and Spock Prime are in the cave and Spock's telling him everything, there's a mention by Kirk of "How is it that I found you in this cave in the middle of an ice planet? It's insane that we should ever even meet this way." Spock says, "Perhaps it's the timestream's way of trying to mend itself. It is fate and destiny trying to bring all of us together."
RO: We're using the rules of quantum mechanics for time travel on this one, as opposed to the classical

Einsteinian rules of relativity. One of the subsets of that theory is that there are multiple universes and that the things that are most probable to happen, happen most often in more universes... So there's more universes out there where Kirk and Spock get together and hang out than not, just because that's what quantum mechanics would say. We were very much playing as much as we could with the latest theories, and trying to tie those into a real sense of destiny. The movie does rely, to some extent for the fans, on a real knowledge of the fact that everyone is going to end up in their proper place.

Live Long and Prosper

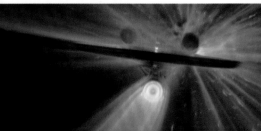

"WE REALIZED THAT WE HADN'T ACTUALLY SEEN ALL THESE CHARACTERS MEET AND GO ON THEIR FIRST ADVENTURE. THAT BECAME AN OBVIOUS PLACE TO EXPLORE."

ALEX KURTZMAN & ROBERTO ORCI

Writer-producers Alexander Hilary Kurtzman and Roberto Gaston Orci went to high school together in Los Angeles. They have been friends and collaborators ever since. Though they attended different institutions of higher education – Mexican-born Orci went to the University of Texas at Austin; L.A. native Kurtzman went to Wesleyan in Middletown, Connecticut – they reunited in the mid-1990s, when the duo cut their professional teeth in television on *Xena: Warrior Princess* and *Hercules: The Legendary Journeys*. From there, they went on to *Jack of All Trades* and *Alias*. It was on *Alias* that they first worked with J.J. Abrams, with whom they would later partner on the feature films *Mission: Impossible III* and *Star Trek*, as well as the TV series *Fringe* – for which the trio received two award nominations from the Writers Guild of America. Orci and Kurtzman also collaborated on 2007's *Transformers* for director Michael Bay, and rejoined forces to write its sequel (with Ehren Kruger), the upcoming *Transformers: Revenge of the Fallen*, as well being assigned to co-write the followup to *Star Trek* with Damon Lindelof – for which they will also reprise their roles as producers.

In July 2007, Orci, a self-described *Star Trek* fan, was named as one of the 50 most powerful Latinos in Hollywood by The Hollywood Reporter.

Eric Bana as Nero

CREATING THE VILLAIN

You've said that you've beefed up the role of Nero in successive drafts. How much did he change?

AK: We went back and forth. We started in our first draft very close to what's in the movie, but before and during the production, we added a whole sequence showing what happens to Nero during the 25 years that he's waiting for Leonard Nimoy's Spock. He was on Rura Penthe in a prison [right]. He and his men had been taken captive by the Klingons. It was all really fun stuff, but we wanted to keep the film at two hours, lean and mean. We ended up going back and editing to make it more of a mystery to where he was.

> "NERO'S ESSENTIALLY A TRUCKER WHOSE WIFE'S BEEN KILLED. WE HAD NEVER THOUGHT OF IT IN THOSE TERMS, BUT I LOVE THAT."

It also keeps the focus clearly on the Bridge crew. Is it fair to call Nero a bit of a McGuffin in this film?

RO: Yes, and that's why Eric Bana is so important to it. He has to do so much and be so soulful with so little, knowing that he is part of helping to support a structure and an origin story that requires an extremely succinct yet effective presence as a villain – and that's what he is.

Klingons, in a scene cut from *Star Trek* (2009)

Both *Star Trek* and *Into Darkness* feature parallels with *The Wrath of Khan*

There are quite a few parallels between Nero and Khan, the villain from *Star Trek II: The Wrath of Khan*. Were they conscious?

RO: Yes, there's a lot of conscious homage to that movie, both in terms of seeing the fact that you see how Kirk solved the *Kobayashi Maru*, which is brought up in that movie, to the theme of whether or not that's cheating, the theme of Kirk and Spock's friendship, that they always shall be friends. This movie is an echo of that.

AK: What always struck us about Khan [above] was that despite the horror of what he did to the entire crew in that movie, when he gives the speech about being marooned on that dead planet, and how he lost his wife and Kirk is responsible for it, you ultimately go, "This is a bad guy with a very understandable personal vendetta." You feel for him in some way. We felt that was a very important thing for Nero: he needed to be a cipher in terms of why he was doing these horrible things, and why he was so interested in Spock, but once the reveal comes, you need to feel the weight of that story on the character. It starts to shift your perception of him.

Bana is so wonderful in the way he comes on the viewscreen and says, "Hi, Christopher, my name's

Nero." You think this is a human being, in some weird way. Even though he's Romulan, you're connecting to him as a person.

RO: We were inspired by Khan for that exactly, but the difference was that Khan was a ruler and a warlord, and this imperial figure. Nero is just a worker from the future.

AK: Someone recently said that he's essentially a trucker whose wife's been killed. We had never thought of it in those terms, but I love that. I think that's great – it's everything we wanted it to be. He's essentially a very normal guy and the idea that normal people can go through these incredible traumas, and become totally different people than they had ever imagined themselves to be is a very sympathetic idea.

Star Trek has certain elements connected to it – and this movie seems to reflect some of the attitudes of the original series, such as no female captains...

RO: I don't think we were too conscious of that, in that we were simply adapting the characters that were from that series as we remember them, for an origin story. If we were having this conversation four movies down the line, which God bless anything like that would ever happen, and we'd continued to do that then perhaps there might be something conscious there. For this, the main crew was Kirk, Spock, Bones, Uhura, Sulu, Scotty, Chekov – and that's what we did. Nothing more complicated than that.

REDEFINING THE CREW

You've added certain wrinkles to the relationships. Was the Spock/Uhura romance something you felt was there all the time, or was it something specific to this timeline version of the characters?

RO: We have sensed an undercurrent of that in some of the episodes that we saw. I think it was a subtext there, but the relationship is certainly unique to this timeline. In the original series, the first interracial kiss ever on television was between Kirk and Uhura, and it seemed that one of the themes we were playing with in this was because it's a changed timeline, what might be some of the fun differences? That was clearly one of the fun differences. What if, instead of the lady's man getting the prize of Uhura's attention, we let it be a way to humanize Spock?

AK: We knew the relationship was going to be controversial but context is everything in those decisions. The reveal that they have been together comes hopefully organically in a moment when Spock is suffering. You have just watched him go through this incredible trauma, and the fact that she's there to comfort him is sort of what the audience wants to do, especially since he can't show emotion – you so desperately want him just to have a hug. When Uhura does that, I think you're taken aback by the choice but also kind of grateful that Spock has a valve for all the emotions he is repressing. We were hopefully pacing the audience into accepting the boldness of that change.

Do you anticipate a backlash from fans?

RO: Not the majority, no. I think most of them will go with it. A 15 per cent vocal minority maybe.

AK: And you can argue context. You may not like the choice, but I think it's done as organically as we could imagine revealing that.

Zoe Saldana as Uhura

Kirk (Chris Pine) in trouble again

The original screen clinch

For the first time, we learn about Jim Kirk's father. As far as you're concerned, what happened in the original timeline? The Kelvin returned to Earth, Winona Kirk delivered Jim in Iowa, and George disappeared off on another ship?

RO: Yes, in the original timeline, we figured they made it back and Kirk was actually born in Iowa, but because the ship was attacked in our movie, he was born prematurely in space, in battle. We thought that was another interesting twist to what was semi-established. If he was born in the cornfields of Iowa once upon a time, the opposite of that is he's born in battle in space.

AK: At one point in conceiving of this, we had thought of naming the ship the *U.S.S. Iowa*. That was going to be our nod to him being born in Iowa, but then we decided that was too radical.

RO: The idea is that his father would have gotten back, and he would have known him for some time as a child – but again, even if we hadn't done this incursion, we could have said that he died when he was eight for all we know.

Did you ever intend to include Christine Chapel?

AK: In our original, original draft we wrote some scenes with Nurse Chapel but ended up losing them. Even in our first draft it's not included. We originally had a flirtation between her and Spock: Nurse Chapel was obviously really obsessed with him and he was not giving her the time of day, which we thought was funny, but then we came onto the Spock/Uhura connection and that's why Nurse Chapel ended up by the wayside.

One character who's noticeably different between the original series and the movie is Captain Pike...

AK: Bruce Greenwood is phenomenal.

Was there pressure for you to include Pike, or did you need a father figure for Jim, and Pike was the right person in the right place?

AK: I think we immediately gravitated toward the idea that we ought to have Pike in the movie without having any context to how we were going to use him.

RO: He seemed to loom large in our minds – the first captain of the *Enterprise*. Who was that? Who was before Kirk? The idea that there could be a first captain before Kirk is a slight romantic mystery that's at the periphery of even some casual fans. It might

Pike (Bruce Greenwood) and (inset) Majel Barrett-Roddenberry as Nurse Chapel

have been [Paramount Pictures executive] Marc Evans who said we had to have Pike in there, and we were immediately like, yeah. Then we found exactly the perfect context for him. We always thought if it was going to be an origin story, then it made sense for Pike to be around, because we were going to see some sort of transition to Kirk as the captain of the *Enterprise*.

AK: It's a funny thing; sometimes the magic puzzle pieces fall into place by themselves. When it started to become a story about how Kirk had lost his father and needed one, it was immediately obvious that Pike was going to become his surrogate father. It never wavered from that. The relationship dynamic wasn't easy to write, but was very clear for us because it just fit.

This is a story of fathers and mothers. You could almost argue there's too much father and mother story in here, but that's kind of the point. Everyone has a father and a mother!

Karl Urban makes an incredible McCoy...
AK: He was one of those amazing casts, in that when he first came in you didn't think he really looked like Bones,

and you couldn't really imagine him as Bones. He was the killer in The *Bourne Ultimatum*, he was in The *Lord of the Rings*, and we had worked with him on *Hercules*. Physically he couldn't be further from DeForest Kelley, but then he started reading – and he became Bones. It was staggering how much he understood intuitively and physically the spirit of Bones. We never looked back.
RO: It was the most surprising transformation.

On a side note, when Jim and Bones meet, where are they going from Riverside?
RO: To San Francisco

So why are they going into space?
RO: Just a suborbital path to get there in five seconds. Or maybe they're taking a long way because they've got to pick up another couple of cadets. They're going suborbital – Hong Kong and then Frisco!

Anton Yelchin has said how much he was channeling Walter Koenig's performance from the original series – but where did the whizzkid side of his character come from?
RO: We picked that up from the original series. If you read the bios and the bible and all that stuff, Chekov was the youngest. I remember reading he was cast to capitalize on The Monkees' Davy Jones' popularity at the time. He was very much supposed to be the youngest one of the crew. We wondered how someone that young got to be there. He had to be a prodigy of some kind. It was a mix of finding out his origin and letting that spring into a character idea.
AK: What Anton does capture with Chekov is that I felt Chekov always seemed very worried. He had worry lines on his forehead! He was always thinking through the problem. I feel like Anton channeled that whole spirit, that whole "Oh, yai yai yai!" That is pure Chekov.

Leonard Nimoy has praised Zachary Quinto's performance, particularly the scene at the Vulcan Science Academy and the way he played "Live long and prosper." Is that how you saw the scene in your minds?
AK: Yes. The parenthetical direction in the script in the dialogue is "(F*** you)". That's exactly what he did.

THE ORIGINAL BEGINNING

Was the intention that Jim and Spock are the same age?
RO: No, they're three or four years apart.

Where did Spock's birth scene come originally?
AK: We shot the scene and ended up losing it for all the right reasons, but the movie originally started with the birth of Spock in terms of the sequencing of their births. Spock was always first because he was four years older, then four years later came Kirk. But because of the way we ended up changing it in post, it does end up feeling like they're the same age. However, when Kirk is taking the *Kobayashi Maru*, you see that Spock designed the test, and he's described as the most esteemed graduate, so you know he's already graduated.

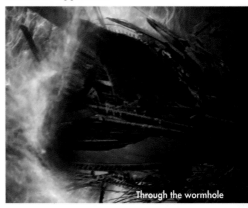
Through the wormhole

So how did the movie originally start?
AK: The original opening was: the Paramount logo of the mountain comes on screen, then the mountain starts to tremble and explodes as it's ripped off into the sky. Suddenly the entire ground of Earth is destroyed – and you realize it's not Earth you're looking at, it's actually Romulus. From that, into the chaos of a planet being destroyed comes the *Jellyfish* being chased by Nero, and they go through time. We never reveal in that original scene scriptwise that it was Spock in the *Jellyfish*. It was more about establishing Nero and why he's chasing the *Jellyfish*. Nero goes through the wormhole, it goes to black, and then you're at the birth of Spock.

> ## "PIKE SEEMED TO LOOM LARGE IN OUR MINDS – THE FIRST CAPTAIN OF THE *ENTERPRISE*. WHO WAS THAT? WHO WAS BEFORE KIRK?"

The point was always to drop the audience in the middle of the story and have them catch up to it. For us as viewers, that's the most fun way to go into a movie, especially a movie about time travel. It just makes the mystery so delicious. We ended up maintaining the spirit of that by starting with the attack on the *Kelvin*. "What is this? Why are they being attacked?" You don't know what's happening rightaway, so you feel like you're trying to catch up to it.

Chris Pine as Kirk

Karl Urban as Bones

AIDING THE DESIGN

How much did you indicate in the script how the Kelvin should look older than the *Enterprise*?

AK: We indicated that it was an older generation ship, so it did not have the same look. In the description, we were setting up when you reveal the *Enterprise* that it is a different class. There was a sense almost that you were starting on the ships from the original series. We wanted to feel that a bit in the texture of the *Kelvin*.

We spent a lot of time describing the feel of the *Narada* because it was going to be something you had never seen on *Trek* before.

RO: But you can never describe what [production designer] Scott [Chambliss] is going to ultimately come up with – he takes it to another level. But we do give a context for it, to give him the goals of what we're thinking, then he runs with it and turns it into his own thing.

AK: We're using adjectives – he's using steels. It's a very different game.

In terms of the timeline, the *Enterprise*'s creation doesn't tally with the original series where Pike's had the *Enterprise* for 11 years when Jim takes it over. In this timeline is it running five years late?

RO: We always tried to figure out what the fan fiction explanation would be, and for that, it would be that after the death of George Kirk, the Riverside shipyards were commemorated in his honor, and that's why there's even a shipyard near his home. The *Kelvin* shuttlecraft escaped with telemetry from their encounter with the ship from the future, so Starfleet's development and construction plans were slightly altered. Hence everything being potentially more advanced, slightly ahead of schedule etc.

Did your scripts simply state that scenes happened on the Bridge of the *Enterprise*, or did you give a description of what you wanted the scenes to look like?

How much day to day input did you have into the Countdown comic book?

RO: We came up with the story. It's very much of a targeted prequel to the movie. The comic book writers are outside of our door just down the hall so it was a "K/O" production. We are doing a lot more stuff, and a lot more *Trek* stuff as well. I'll leave it to our comic partners to discuss that.

How much were you involved with Alan Dean Foster's novelization?

RO: We had a great meeting with him. He read the script and he said "When I read things, I have to be honest with my criticisms," and he gave his couple of well-thought *Trek* notes, but he said, "Don't worry – I'll help you cover some of these gaps in the book." He's done *Transformers* as well, but we'd never actually met before, so to finally get to sit down with him, and him being an amazing sci-fi writer on his own, the idea that he would cover our screenplay was great.

Would you be interested in annotating a version of the screenplay for publication?

RO: That's a good idea, I'm sure they'll do that.

Looking forward to the sequel, how far are you with ideas for it?

AK: We have some ideas.

RO: We've talked about it very informally over a glass of wine here or there, but we haven't really dived in because we're waiting for this experience to come to closure, and really see what fans in particular think work and didn't work.

> ## "THE REASON THAT WE DID IT WAS BECAUSE *STAR TREK* MEANS AS MUCH TO THE FANS AS IT ALWAYS HAS TO US, AND TO KNOW THAT THEY FELT WE DID THEM PROUD IS DEFINITELY THE WHOLE ENCHILADA."

Has there been anything in the reactions so far to the movie that you weren't expecting?

RO: I'm always surprised when anybody likes anything!

What's been the most rewarding part of doing this for you?

AK: The night we screened the movie in Austin was the first time we had seen the movie with an audience. I was sitting with Leonard Nimoy on my right, Bob next to Leonard, and Damon Lindelof on my left – and there was this very intense moment of the different generations of *Trek* coming together for the fans that everybody has made this movie for. Hearing the fans alternate between applause, some crying and a lot of laughter, and having people come up to us afterwards literally in tears because they were so grateful: we didn't expect that reaction. The reason that we did it was because *Star Trek* means as much to them as it always has to us, and to know that they felt we did them proud is definitely the whole enchilada.

RO: Hear hear! ⚙

RO: We were faithful to their positions and the basic shape of the layout but certainly we knew that the Bridge was going to be something that would require all hands on deck in order to be able to conceptualize. I don't know that we spent hours poring over every detail of describing the Bridge.

AK: We gave broad strokes, but we can't take any credit away from Scott and his brilliant design team. It is one of the most brilliantly production-designed movies that I've seen in a really long time.

The fleet in tatters

The *Enterprise* under construction

CHRIS HEMSWORTH IS
GEORGE KIRK

The *U.S.S. Kelvin*

George Kirk
(Hemsworth)

Wearing tight lycra for the first time was just one of the many new sensations that Australian actor Chris Hemsworth experienced during his work on *Star Trek*, playing the helmsman of the *U.S.S. Kelvin*, George Samuel Kirk...

Two key players in the *Star Trek* saga have never been seen on screen before – indeed little beyond their existence has been revealed. James Tiberius Kirk's parents, George and Winona Kirk, are the central figures of the early part of the new *Star Trek* movie, as the *U.S.S. Kelvin*, carrying a heavily pregnant Winona Kirk (played by *House* star Jennifer Morrison) on board, encounters the Narada.

To play George Kirk, J.J. Abrams turned to Australian actor Chris Hemsworth, who had only been working in America for a few months. "I'd been shooting for a couple of months in Chicago," he recalls, "and the day after I got back to L.A., I was running around town in a bunch of meetings. I had a phone call from my manager saying that I needed to drive across right away to Paramount Studios and meet J.J. Abrams in his office to do the scene. I cancelled what I was doing, drove over there, did the scene in his office at his desk and he said, 'Fantastic – we have to work together. You start next week.' And that was it!"

Abrams didn't share very much with Hemsworth at this stage, but unlike some of his cast mates, the actor did use a genuine scene from the film for his audition. "It was all very secretive," the actor recalls. "The scene changed a little bit by the time we were shooting it, but it was definitely some of what I was going to shoot."

Hemsworth had very little time to prepare for the role, although there wasn't very much he could do anyway. "I feel like *Star Trek* has been something you always know about, whether you're an avid fan or not," he explains. "It's gone on for so long, and there's so much of it. But it wasn't something I watched – it wasn't in the circles I grew up in when I was younger. But I certainly had an immense respect for what it had achieved. It has been very big in Australia – I remember a friend of mine's dad was really into it, and had wall to wall videotapes of the show at his house. I think J.J. wanted to pay homage to what had been done, but also create a fresh spin on it – something that will please the previous fans, but maybe create a new audience as well."

Since George Kirk was an entirely new creation, actor and director could collaborate on how he would appear. "On set we discussed how we wanted to play it," he says. "J.J. had very specific ideas about

what we wanted to achieve, but he's also the kind of director that gives you the freedom to try other things and put your own interpretation on it. It was more a case of taking the scenes that we had, and finding the truth in what was being said, then just playing that and trusting in the overall picture J.J. was creating and that the writers had done for us."

Piecing together a back story for his own character, Hemsworth feels that George Kirk is "someone who has quite a strong sense of justice. He's that old-fashioned kind of good guy: he has strong morals and puts other people before himself. But he was also played as someone in his mid-20s. He's still quite young, so I think a lot of who he is was ingrained, maybe through his upbringing. I feel like he had a pretty strong sense of character, and especially to be put in the position he is at such a young age says a lot about who he is."

Hemsworth makes a big impact as Jim Kirk's father, George

Hemsworth was pleased that his scenes featured a lot of "solid human interactions. J.J. said to me at one point that the interaction between George and his wife could be in any war, on a ship or a tank. It didn't have to be looked at as *Star Trek* or an 'outer space, other world' thing. He said that he wanted these people to be real human beings, and their interactions to be relatable to anybody. That's a big strength of his, and certainly his focus. I remember watching an interview with him about *Mission: Impossible III* and him saying that he wanted to know where Ethan Hunt lived and what kind of person he was when he went home. That's what J.J. likes to do: take these larger than life characters, yet make them still human and accessible to the audience."

In many ways, Hemsworth was relieved that he didn't have a long time to contemplate what he was letting himself in for. "That was funny," he says. "In a really good

> "THERE WERE A COUPLE OF TIMES WHEN I WAS SITTING THERE ON SET, AND I THOUGHT THAT IT DOESN'T GET ANY BIGGER THAN THIS... AND I WONDERED WHAT I WAS DOING THERE!"

way, I was thankful for not having enough time to think about it, because the turnaround from the audition to when I was shooting was so quick. I didn't have too much time to think about the pressure that was built around it. But afterward, the more I heard about it, I started hoping I did an okay job!"

There wasn't much rehearsal time. "I remember meeting Jennifer Morrison who said, 'Hey, Chris, I think we're married and I'm pregnant. How are you?' and off we went. That's the nature of this business.

"There were a couple of times when I was sitting there on set, and I thought that it doesn't get any bigger than this, in terms of money, expertise and everything that's put into making a film. And I wondered what I was doing there! But the great thing about J.J. is he just instills such confidence in you because the vision he has is so strong. During filming, any moments of doubt are reassured with his strength and the type of personality he has.

"J.J. really embodies a leader quality," he continues, "He knows what he wants in all areas, and he knows everyone. He's accessible to anyone on set, any other human being involved. He's not standoffish or picky about who he hangs with. He's just the most normal human being and that's incredible for someone in his position. The guy is a genius from every angle – knowing how to direct actors and say the right things to get what he wants, getting ideas for shots and how to play the scene. The fact that he's such a great person is kind of insulting – he has the complete package!"

Hemsworth was equally in awe of the crew working on the film. "They were such great people, a hell of a lot of fun," he says. "They're such a tight crew. They've worked on previous films together, and they have that well-oiled machine feel. It was something really special to be part of – I'd only been over in the States for all of four months at that stage, so it was mind-blowing and exciting." A

George Kirk takes command

CHRIS HEMSWORTH

Chris Hemsworth was born in Melbourne, Australia but was raised on nearby Philip Island. When he was five, his family moved to an Aboriginal Community for five years. After returning to Melbourne he pursued an acting career, beginning with guest spots on local series *Guinevere Jones*, *Marshall Law*, *The Saddle Club* and *Fergus McPhail*, eventually earning a regular role as Kimberly Jonathan Hyde on soap opera *Home and Away*. He moved to Sydney for the show and quickly became a teen heartthrob, staying with the series from 2004 through summer 2007. His work was recognized by his peers with two Logie Award nominations, winning one in 2005 for Most Popular New Talent. He has subsequently been on the Australian edition of *Dancing with the Stars*, partnered with Abbey Ross, but was eliminated after six rounds. He made his film debut in *Root of All Evil*, which has yet to be released, and followed *Star Trek* by reteaming with Eric Bana for *A Perfect Getaway* which opened in early Spring 2009.

Recommended performance:
Hemsworth is now best known for portraying Marvel superhero Thor.
Kimberly Hyde: Home and Away

KIRK

CHRIS PINE

Main photos © Zade Rosenthal

Before taking on the iconic role of Captain James Tiberius Kirk in 2009's *Star Trek*, Chris Pine had appeared in TV shows from *ER* to *Six Feet Under*, by way of *CSI: Miami*. Soon to be seen as the new *Jack Ryan*, his Hollywood star is definitely in the ascendant. Shortly before *Star Trek Into Darkness* was about to hit cinemas, Pine talked to Tara Bennett about returning to the Bridge of the *Enterprise*.

You've had a few years with the Kirk character on your resumé now, so has your life changed in unexpected ways since *Star Trek*?

Chris Pine: Yeah, definitely. Professionally, it opened up a lot of doors. It gave me a lot of opportunities I hadn't had before I signed up to do the films. There's a decrease in anonymity, but it's always nice to hear people shout your name, and people enjoyed the first film. Things have definitely changed, but it's all welcome stuff.

Do you consider Kirk the most loaded role you've done?

When we all first signed up to do it, and began making the first film, J.J.'s prescription to us was that it was our job to make our characters specific and unique to us, which was nice to hear because, obviously, there are many, many years, and many stories that other actors have already done in these iconic roles, with these iconic characters. Hearing that gave us freedom to take as much as we wanted from what our predecessors had done, and to run with whatever we thought was necessary to bring

"KIRK MIGHT HAVE GOTTEN THE CAPTAIN'S CHAIR IN THE FIRST ONE, BUT IN THE SECOND ONE HE HAS TO EARN THE CAPTAIN'S CHAIR."

Kirk: armed and ready

CAREER NOTES

TELEVISION
ER (2003)
The Guardian (2003)
CSI: Miami (2003)
American Dreams (2004)
Six Feet Under (2005)

FILMS
The Princess Diaries 2: Royal Engagement (2004)
Just My Luck (2006)
Smokin' Aces (2006)
Unstoppable (2010)
This Means War (2012)
Rise of the Guardians (2012)
Jack Ryan (2013)
Mantivities (2014)

our characters to life. I think of Kirk as less of an iconic character and more as a character given to me on the written page. I used my script as my "bible", and tried to make sense from that. I also tried not to do Bill [Shatner], because he obviously made an incredible mark on this character, but I thought it was necessary to pay tribute to that.

In *The Captains* (Shatner's entertaining and enlightening documentary), you talked with Bill about infusing your Kirk with some of his performance attributes, to create a subtle connection. What did you use?

"THE FACT THAT KIRK IS THE CAPTAIN OF THIS SHIP, AND IS GOING THROUGH A MAJOR EXISTENTIAL CRISIS, DOES NOT BODE WELL."

For me, watching the original series, it was really his sense of humor. I thought he was incredibly funny. Often times he was doing

comedy that I think was maybe going over people's heads, and people mistook for hammy. But I think he is such a finely skilled actor, with a fine sense of the absurd and a sense of his own self, which he used to great effect many years later playing Denny Crane, on *Boston Legal*. So that, to me, was what I really, really enjoyed about his performance. It was something in this new incarnation that we all talked with J.J. about, the use of levity and the fact that, as dark as some of our stuff is in this new film, we always have time to smile and make people laugh.

Kirk, Scotty and Bones assess the situation in sickbay

Kirk receives some words of wisdom from Admiral Pike

How did Shatner entice you to be part of *The Captains*?
His producer worked out at the same gym that I did. I first heard about it that way. (*Laughs*) He had pitched this bit that we ended up doing, with the arm-wrestling, and I told my publicists to let his people know that I was happy to do a sit-down interview but I wasn't really interested in doing any kind of 'bit'. And then on the day, Bill comes into my room, and he has all these notes written on napkins and note cards. He was so excited about this whole thing, and it's virtually impossible to say no to the man when he's there, acting out every little beat in our wrestling match. He was directing it in the room. I hadn't spent as much time with him alone as I did that day of the interview. He's an interesting, funny, charismatic man. I was quite taken by what a good interviewer he was. First of all, I thought it was kind of ridiculous my doing it. Everybody else involved had years playing these characters. I felt like some kind of poser on *Inside the Actor's Studio* or something, but it was fun, and we had a good time doing it.

Speaking of feedback, was there any advice about playing Kirk that stuck with you as you started the sequel?
Once J.J. gave us the script, it all made sense. Really, what he kept stressing in the second one was the fact that Kirk might have gotten the Captain's chair in the first one, but in the second one he has to earn the Captain's chair. What does it mean to be a leader? In the first one, he became one very quickly and accidentally. In the second one, he finds himself growing up

very fast, becoming an adult very fast. The bravado he does so well in the first film, in the second maybe isn't the best quality or color with which to lead these men and women into battle. It's really about humility, and maturity, and growing up in a couple of hours.

Obviously the media was bugging you for years about the sequel, but what was the secret development process like for you? Did you check in with J.J. along the way, or did you just get the script?
It's really J.J.'s show. He's the master magician behind everything. There were a couple years

when he went off and did other things. I would hear trickles through the information grapevine, through [writers] Damon (Lindelof) or Alex (Kurtzman), what they were thinking about for the second one. But I knew nothing until I got to read the script, under lock and key, in one of the producer's offices. So, we very much await J.J.'s orders, and once it begins it's a much more collaborative experience.

It's a lot of fun to be able to come to set, as scary as it is that things may be changing a lot, as Alex, Bob (Orci) and J.J. figure things out, and what might work better. It's also very exciting to see how these

Kirk and Spock take their crew *Into Darkness*

Kirk faces danger on the *Enterprise*

minds that came from television – which happens so fast, and where they had to be nimble and on their toes, and nothing was precious – it's fascinating to see how they work in the shorthand they have, and to be included in conversations about what might happen to the character, where he should go, and how a line might affect X, Y, and Z.

What initially stood out to you about *Star Trek Into Darkness*?

The sheer scale of it. There's a lot of destruction, and a lot of explosions. The fact that Kirk is the Captain of this ship, and is going through a major existential crisis, does not bode well for where the crew and the *Enterprise* find themselves in the middle of this picture. It's really exciting, because in any great epic story, you want it to go from A–Z and back again, and this has so many different colors. It has the excitement, it has moments of levity, it has the romance. A big, steaming apple pie of all sorts of great things.

When you got ready to don the uniform again for *Into Darkness*, how did it feel: less nerve-wracking or more because of the success of the first one?

It was actually a little more nerve-wracking the second time around. Any sophomore outing for an artist is like, "Man! We did a good job, and now people are expecting more!" The first one was much easier, because there was almost an expectation of failure, so there was that wonderful position of being the underdog and saying, "Wait until you see what we have up our sleeve." To J.J.'s credit, and I've said it a thousand times, he knows how to cast well, and he's a great general. When you come on set, he makes the actor, the grip, the craft service person feel like a part of one big family, making something special. Then it just becomes about the scene. It might be on the Bridge of the *Enterprise*, but it's just another day, and another scene, trying to make it the best.

Where is Kirk in relation to his crew at the start of this new story?

It's a bunch of young kids newly thrown together, still trying to figure themselves and their relationships out. I think there is a [different] dynamic between these characters, and who they trust, between the original

Kirk faces his enigmatic nemesis, John Harrison

"HARRISON'S ABILITY TO LASER IN ON KIRK'S INSECURITIES, AND MAGNIFY THEM, AND THEN MIRROR THEM BACK AT HIM, IS TERRIBLY FRIGHTENING FOR KIRK."

series and these films. For instance, [Shatner's] Kirk is the man of action, and the man who trusts his gut but knows it's better and wiser to defer to the logic of Spock on occasion. This Kirk is still trying to figure the best way to lead, and who his consigliores are, and who it's wisest to trust. They're not quite there yet, but they are moving toward that, and I think it makes for an interesting story.

Where are Kirk and Spock in this film? Still as contentious as in the first?

I would say the defining feature of these two characters – with Spock being a man of logic, reason, and who works well in a system, and our version of Kirk who is a bit more rebellious, follows his heart, is way more emotional, and doesn't work best in a system – they come to a head in this film, in a way that allows these two characters to learn much more about one another, to respect one another's perspectives on the world, and to more fully realize who they are.

Trek has some great villains, so how is Benedict Cumberbatch's John Harrison meant to test Kirk?

To break him down. Benedict's character is able to cut Kirk down to size. This arrogant man at the beginning of the film, who thinks he can do anything, quickly realizes that he can't. He realizes he's not the smartest, not the fastest, not the ballsiest, not the strongest, and he finds himself on his knees, very, very scared. I think Harrison's ability to laser in on Kirk's insecurities, and magnify them, and then mirror them back at him, is terribly frightening for Kirk, as he finds himself in the middle of this storm.

Having seen the finished film, what's surprised you most?

It's probably that this film manages to fulfill people's expectations of what a tent-pole summer movie should be, which in the past five years has become quite a feat in terms of spectacle. There are certain things we had to do to satisfy a modern audience's craving for that. I think we hit it out of the park. The action sequences are spectacular. People can expect to see something fantastic. We also married that with what people love about *Star Trek*, which are complex, human dramas. I think we have that going for us. Also, this cast is a really tight group, off-set. Hopefully that kind of friendship, and bond, will seep into this film. It's that final patina in a film about a bunch of characters you are watching, where you really believe they care about one another. We do. We have a great time and hopefully that love found its way into the film. ▲

MICHAEL KAPLAN

COSTUME DESIGNER

As with many of the behind the camera personnel on *Star Trek*, costume designer Michael Kaplan initially thought that his lack of familiarity with the franchise would be a disadvantage – but his fresh approach revitalized the 1960s originals, while still honoring the original William Ware Theiss designs...

Michael Kaplan was on holiday in Massachusetts in summer 2007 when he got the call from his agent telling him that director J.J. Abrams "very much wanted" to meet him with regard to the multi-million dollar revival of *Star Trek*. "J.J. was in Maine, finishing up his summer holiday," Kaplan recalls, "so I flew up there, and we had a meeting in a coffee shop."

The renowned designer jokes that Abrams had had so much to deal with that they had almost forgotten about hiring a costume designer and remembers telling the director that he wasn't sure if he was the right person for the job, since he "definitely wasn't a Trekkie."

"I wasn't well versed in the *Star Trek* jargon," he explains, "and I wasn't a fan. I wasn't really somebody who followed the series. I didn't know that much about it – I hadn't seen any of the *Star Trek* movies, although, of course I grew up with the TV series and saw a few episodes. I wanted him to know that I would have to do a lot of research into the series."

But that wasn't what Abrams was looking for. "He told me that since it was a prequel, he wanted to honor certain things, but it was uncharted territory. It was good that I wasn't that knowledgeable about *Star Trek*: he thought that would be a plus, and I would be bringing something fresh to it."

At the end of the hour long conversation, Abrams invited Kaplan on board. There was no time to waste. "It was late August, and we started shooting in November," Kaplan points out. "There was very little prep time. I hit the ground running, and put together an entire department. It was almost like the old Hollywood studio system: we created the whole department on the Paramount lot. We thought that in the long run, it would save time, rather than having to go to different shops and farm the work out."

The sheer scale of the production – with hundreds of extras for the Starfleet Academy scenes to be clothed, as well as the crews of the *U.S.S. Kelvin* and the *U.S.S. Enterprise* – of course meant that some of the work had to be mass produced. "We did prototypes in our Wardrobe Department, then farmed them out," Kaplan says. "But a lot of the individual stuff was turned out of that custom department on the Paramount lot. It was very exciting to have all those people employed like they used to in old Hollywood."

CONCLUDED ON P.44

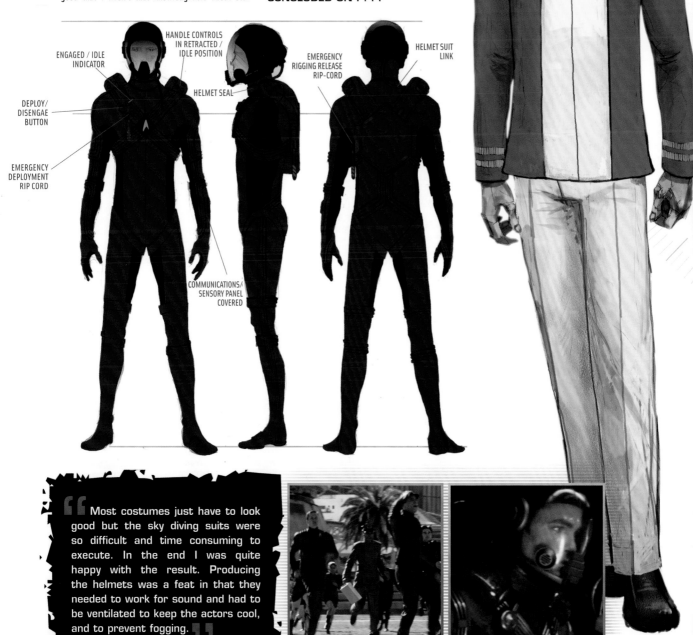

ENGAGED / IDLE INDICATOR

HANDLE CONTROLS IN RETRACTED / IDLE POSITION

HELMET SEAL

EMERGENCY RIGGING RELEASE RIP-CORD

HELMET SUIT LINK

DEPLOY/ DISENGAE BUTTON

EMERGENCY DEPLOYMENT RIP CORD

COMMUNICATIONS/ SENSORY PANEL COVERED

"Most costumes just have to look good but the sky diving suits were so difficult and time consuming to execute. In the end I was quite happy with the result. Producing the helmets was a feat in that they needed to work for sound and had to be ventilated to keep the actors cool, and to prevent fogging."

U.S.S. KELVIN

This page shows two of the three color-coded uniforms (the missing color is pearl grey) for the Kelvin crew. "I wanted the audience to feel the time difference between the *Kelvin* and the *Enterprise*, so I did research into sci fi movies of the 1950s. I did something that had that kind of period future feeling to it. It feels a little retro in its futurism."

This fit with the retro look given to the *Kelvin*'s Bridge and Engine Room by production designer Scott Chambliss. "Scott and I would compare our designs and they'd fit together even before we spoke about them. We were definitely on the same wavelength."

"I WANTED THE AUDIENCE TO FEEL THE TIME DIFFERENCE BETWEEN THE *KELVIN* AND THE *ENTERPRISE,* SO I DID RESEARCH INTO SCI FI MOVIES OF THE 1950S."

23RD CENTURY FASHIONS

J.J. liked the idea of Chris Pine wearing some sort of an equivalent to a T-shirt, jeans and leather jacket. What we came up satisfied that need – we weren't really trying to make him look futuristic for the sake of it. We didn't really want the costumes to take over. We liked that 'angry young man' James Dean quality. If you put too much period detail, it would be too much of a statement – we wanted Chris to just look good, and be appropriate in the future time, and not be looking at the details of his clothes."

" We didn't really want to create futuristic clothes just to make a statement. We wanted them to be futuristic but not really that noticeable. "

STARFLEET ACADEMY

The women had lots of different options for the cadet uniforms. "They could wear pants, skirt and sweater, a skirt and jacket, or a jumper – an over-sweater like a little dress. That's pretty much what Uhura wore, the jumper. We loved the idea of sticking to the homage to the 1960s and putting the girls into mini-skirts. Zoe Saldana is adorable – it was so much fun to dress her. She has such a great figure for short skirts and the costume – she was the main prototype for the costumes."

> **J.J. was crazy about the Academy uniform costume but they were so hard to mass produce. There were hundreds and hundreds, all requiring much hand-work to fit correctly.**

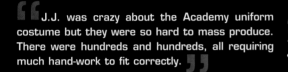

Michael Kaplan

A celebrated movie costume designer for close to 30 years, Philadelphian Michael Kaplan earned the 1983 award for Best Costume Design for his work in *Blade Runner*, from the British Academy of Film and Television Arts. He has also been nominated in the 1999 Saturn Awards for *Armageddon*; in the 2000 Costume Designers Guild Awards for *Fight Club*; and in the 2006 CDG Awards for *Mr. & Mrs Smith*. Kaplan also contributed to such films as *Flashdance*, *Malice*, *Se7en*, *Pearl Harbor*, *Panic Room*, and *I am Legend* before being tapped for *Star Trek*. His work will also be seen in the upcoming *The Sorcerer's Apprentice* and *Motherless Brooklyn*.

In addition to costume design and fashion styling for the Hollywood film industry, Kaplan works on still shoots, music videos, and TV commercials. He also does editorial work for the magazines *W*, *Italian Vogue*, and *L'Uomo Vogue*.

As an actor, Kaplan made brief appearances in *Armageddon*, *Saved By the Bell: The New Class*, and an episode of *Seinfeld*.

"Since the end of the movie is the start of the entire TV *Star Trek*, I didn't want to do something radically different. I wanted to stay very close to the original design, but update it.

"I had the *Star Trek* logo done in an optical repeat pattern on the fabric, in the same color as the fabric, but a little bit darker, so it made a texture. When you look very closely, you can see it's the logo created in a repeat.

"In the original series, the costumes were all in one point but now there is an undershirt and an over-shirt. The undershirt is a black semi-mock turtle neck, and then the colored shirt goes over that. The shirt Kirk wears for the majority of the movie is just the undershirt. It does have the logo embossed on the left side of the chest in the same color very subtlely.

"The rank is on the sleeve. That was a new process of heat transferred mylar, depending on the number of stripes they have.

"I thought the pants would be almost like futuristic blue jeans. There's detailing in the knees for movement, and they're made in a dark charcoal gray twill fabric.

"We got some basic boots and then our special effects craft department 'futurized' them, because we needed thousands of them.

"Everything else that anyone wears was specially made to order."

VULCAN

"Although I started from scratch, I tried for the same sort of feel as seen before, without copying or duplicating anything, and simplifying everything. Oftentimes, in futuristic movies they would look back to Ancient Rome, Greece or Egypt and have men coming out in togas or things that gladiators would wear. I wanted to stay away from that kind of future. I never really understood why people do things like that in futuristic movies, so we avoided long robes and sandals totally. I wanted the clothes to look like they made sense for a futuristic society without being too cumbersome."

"Amanda, Spock's mother, is wearing a headscarf because she was "rescued" at home by Spock's father on his motorcycle [when Vulcan is on the brink of destruction]. When we shot it the long scarf looked fantastic blowing in the wind. The strange shape of the corset made sense when we saw other Vulcan scenes with other women shaped the same. These scenes were cut out in the editing process. "

"The Vulcan 'school uniforms' were inspired by a design by the revolutionary 1960s fashion designer Rudy Gernreich (a true genius). His muse and model, Peggy Moffatt, even looked (and looks) like a Vulcan! "

NERO AND THE ROMULANS

"They were like futuristic pirates. We didn't see them wearing uniforms, although there was a uniformity to what they wore. Each person's clothes were different: they were very distressed and almost feeling a little bit barbaric.

"Those costumes I had made in Bali – I was at a flea market one day, and saw somebody selling clothes that they had made in Bali, and I liked the way they had treated the fabrics, and a lot of the distressing and stitching. I said to the guy, 'If I do some designs up, would you be interested in working on a film building my designs? There's a lot of craftsmanship that I would like to do, and if you can mass produce it, I think it can save us a lot of time and energy trying to translate it to somebody here who has never done that kind of work.' He agreed to do it, and we formed a partnership: he went back to Bali, and took the designs. That was really scary because of the time he had to manufacture the fabric and the costumes. But it all came together in the end."

> "Nero's costume was trimmed with fish skins and faux monkey fur."

SPOCK PRIME

"Of course I wanted to please Leonard Nimoy, and he was not a pushover! I had to tell him why I was doing things. I wanted his character to have an elegance about him, a senior statesman. The clothes were very regal and simple. You don't see very much of them – he's often in shadow in the film, or in close-up but you feel the regalness of what he's wearing. There's also a consistency between what he wears and everyone else from his planet."

"Spock Prime's snowsuit was so much fun to design. The hood was quite a challenge: I drew it first, and then figured out how to build it, with the help of some brilliant costume makers. The coat is metalicized leather, the spherical hood is fur-lined. The hood is a hardened globe which is held in place with magnets, and collapses into a collar when pulled apart by the wearer.

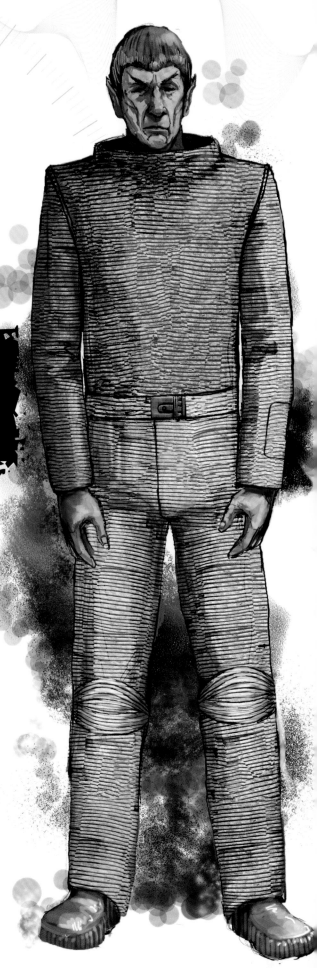

Spock Prime in the elegant look I created for Vulcan business attire. All the Council Members wear versions of this draped suit. The fabrics are slightly metallic; the jackets are slightly asymmetrical: almost half suit, half toga. Mr. Nimoy loved this costume.

"OF COURSE I WANTED TO PLEASE LEONARD NIMOY, AND HE WAS NOT A PUSHOVER!"

CONTINUED FROM P.36

Looking back, Kaplan admits that the lack of time on the project was the biggest challenge that he and his team faced. "We started so late we never really caught up," he admits. "We were always doing things for the next day – having fittings at the last minute and getting the clothes there just in time. It was very stressful! But you can't hold up the camera, and I don't think we ever did. It was a huge undertaking with the sheer numbers of people in different workshops at Paramount and throughout the city."

However, Kaplan was delighted when J.J. Abrams told him that he "really surpassed his vision. He was really pleased, and you can't ask for more than that. He was very happy with the balance between the homage I did to the TV series and the freshness and newness of it. That's what he was looking for.

"When people see a movie, they don't know the pressures you're under, and for J.J. to still be happy with the outcome of the film, with everything fitting in, not being overpowering but just on the right level, pleases me."

DAN MINDEL
DIRECTOR OF PHOTOGRAPHY

For *Star Trek*, J.J. Abrams gathered together many of the team that had worked with him on *Mission: Impossible III* – including its Director of Photography, Dan Mindel...

How early did you get involved with *Star Trek*?
When I heard J.J. was going to be doing it, I made it known that I'd like to work on it. Once they had the Art Department up and running they invited me along to scout and give them my tuppence worth.

What were your first thoughts in terms of what the look of the film should be?
I assumed that it was going to be visually based upon the films and the TV series that ran before it, but it became obvious very quickly that J.J. didn't want to do that. He said to us that we should really not refer to anything other than the overall feel of the series, not the movies, and then we would come up with our own interpretation of that, which we did.

My first thought as always was that I wanted to

photograph it anamorphically to give it a big-screen feel. I saw the other movies through my lifetime and didn't really think that they had escaped the TV feel. Just by nature, they were dated, and we wanted to contemporize *Star Trek* in such a way that the youngsters who had never seen or heard of it would be engaged.

J.J. is a master at that. His contemporization of these monolithic enterprises is fantastic. He's one of the directors out there with his finger on the pulse of the popular zeitgeist. He can interpret what younger people are looking for. I'm confident all these new kids are going to see *Star Trek* and go nuts.

We started from a very open pallet, and zeroed in. It took a while to get to how we were going to make this look but once we had shot film tests, it became obvious straightaway. The first question anyone asks

is how much is it going to cost? That becomes the overriding concern for the studio and the producers. I had persuaded J.J. to shoot widescreen for *Mission: Impossible*, and when we started this movie I said it really should be shot the same way, and done analog, not digitally. He said, "Prove it," so that's what we did. It becomes about an aesthetic, as opposed to the technical side of things. We were able to show him the aesthetic I wanted by getting people in wardrobe and bits of set, shooting them the way we wanted, then projecting them with him saying which bits he liked.

That took a long time! J.J. is a huge multi-tasker, so for us to get him on consecutive days was not really doable. It probably took a month to lock in the type of equipment we were going to use, and once that was done, we just waited for the make-up, hair and wardrobe to be developed and designed, and then prior to starting principal photography, we shot tests with the new actors as well as with Leonard Nimoy, and looked at them on film.

Designer Scott Chambliss told us that the shape of the Bridge was dictated by the anamorphic shooting. Were there other considerations that you asked him to take into account?
Not really. Scott already had the conceptual designs done, so when I saw the rough schematics, three quarters of the issues were already solved. I could see what he was thinking. What we decided to do was let him design the sets with the lighting built in, and we gave his department one of our lighting guys who could be onboard for the whole of their process. Every time they had a design issue he could answer it, so when the sets were built, all our issues had already been dealt with. We came along and shot the sets without too much disassembly – we didn't have to explode the sets and take the walls out, which is how J.J. likes to work.

On the *Narada*, did each different configuration produce different problems?
We had incredibly detailed models built beforehand and we were able to play around with them on the table top. I had a rough plan in place for the overall scheme of how it was going to be lit, but for each change around, we adapted at ground level at the time. That was a much easier way of working because I could see what I had to do in front of me.

It gave us a bit of fear before we started, because it's not really a conventional way of shooting a movie – that's more of a theatrical, stage set. I approached it from that point of view: it was a set with depth to it, as you would get in a theatre. In the end, it worked pretty well.

The very important thing to J.J. was to give all the sets scale. He wanted them to feel huge, because we realized from the movies and the TV shows that there was very little scale to everything.

Was there a different aesthetic to the shooting of the ships from the two different time periods?

Kirk takes off

Inside the *Narada*

We shot the *Kelvin* scenes first, and that was a trial run as far as I was concerned for how we were going to shoot the *Enterprise*. I knew that how the *Enterprise* looked and felt was going to be the most important part of the movie. We went onto the *Kelvin* set knowing that we were going to be blind for the first few days until we started seeing dailies from those sets, then we could take notes and add whatever we wanted to for the *Enterprise*, which hadn't been built yet.

We wanted to make the *Kelvin* a lot darker and less welcoming and positive than the *Enterprise* was going to be, so everything is muted in there. It is in a really sticky situation in the story anyway, so it deteriorates very quickly in front of your eyes! It does feel like it is in distress.

Technologically speaking, the *Enterprise* was so many years ahead it was going to be easy to give it a visual difference, but what we had to do was translate the feel so that when the viewer first sees the Bridge, they go, "Oh my god, that is fantastic."

Scott and I discussed how the surfaces in the ships were going to have the sorts of surfaces that you'd find in cars built in Detroit in the 1970s: a lot of chrome and beautifully finished dashboards that weren't plastic. They were all curvy and beautiful.

I always like sets to have a lot of reflections and moving lights, and all those kinds of things to give them an atmosphere and an energy. We designed the *Enterprise* to be all sparkly and glistening. Whenever you saw anything, it had an almost halo or shininess to it, which I think you can see in the movie.

"THE VERY IMPORTANT THING TO J.J. WAS TO GIVE ALL THE SETS SCALE."

Vulcan under fire

Both engine rooms were shot on location – how much input did you have into the choice of location?

A huge amount but it comes down to that dirty word, money. What usually happens is the director comes along and says "I love this place; this is a dream," and asks if I can make it work. My first answer is always, "Yes, we can do it." How we can do it is something we'll find out later when I bring the technical guys with me to take a look. We then do a budget for the producers to say how much equipment and crew that we'll need to make it work, and they say yes or no. If directors say they have to have a place, nine times out of 10 they'll get it.

The Vulcan sequences were shot at Vasquez Rock which has turned up before in *Star Trek* [right]. Did you look back at how it's been used before to do something differently, or just approach it as a location for this film?

A little bit of both. I was absolutely certain that I didn't want it to look like *Planet of the Apes*. As long as it didn't do that, I was going to be fine. The amount of CG we were going to do was going to convey a whole bevy of terrible images.

How do you work with the visual effects team to coordinate your efforts?

Computer generated effects can lack a certain spontaneity so it can just look like what it is. J.J. and I like to bury the CG in organic images so it doesn't appear like CG. While you're building solar systems and planets, it's inescapable in certain ways, but for the everyday use of CG you can cover it, and that's what we'd really try to do. We consulted with our visual effects producer, a genius (and an Englishman to boot), Roger Guyett, who we've worked with before. We understand his needs.

I have a great relationship with Roger: we'd talk about a location or a set, and what was required from him by J.J., and then I would help him by putting him in the best position technically so that he can make me look good! It works really well when we do that, because the effects are blended in very well and generally look like they live there. That's a very J.J. requirement: the construction and feel of these things should not be so much in your face so you sit back going, "There's another digital set." What we try to do is put them in the background – if you see it, you see it; if you don't, you don't. Either way, they feel natural.

> ## "SELLING THE ILLUSION OF WHAT IS GOING ON IS PART OF MAKING A MOVIE, AND SO MUCH IS LOW-TECH, REALLY SIMPLE STUFF!"

Do you use a similar approach for the stunt sequences?

Part of making movies is illusion. People from Charlie Chaplin and Buster Keaton to J.J. over the last hundred years have been using the same tricks over and over again – and they work. We all take tremendous pleasure out of performing those tricks. Selling the illusion of what is going on is part of making a movie, and so much is low-tech, really simple stuff! But it's efficient.

The sky dive sequence is something we talked about in depth for many weeks, but when it came down to shooting it, it was nuts and bolts and string, stuff that you just wouldn't believe. The finished article is

Original series episode "Arena"

A familiar location

DANIEL MINDEL

Cinematographer Daniel Mindel's life and career span the globe. Born in South Africa, then educated in Australia and the United Kingdom, Mindel was an assistant camera for British director John Boorman on the 1985 feature *The Emerald Forest*, before later transitioning to the United States. He is best known for his frequent collaborations throughout the 1990s with directors Ridley Scott (*Thelma and Louise, White Squall, G.I. Jane*) and Tony Scott (*Crimson Tide, Enemy of the State, Spy Game,* and *Domino*). Mindel appears in the documentary short, *Bounty Hunting on Acid: Tony Scott's Visual Style*. His other noteworthy film credits include *The Bourne Identity* and *The Skeleton Key*. Prior to *Star Trek*, Mindel worked with J.J. Abrams as director of photography on *Mission: Impossible III*.

A dynamic scene in the *Enterprise* corridors

"*STAR TREK* HAD TO HAVE INTEGRITY: IT NEEDED THE WEIGHT, THE BALLAST AND THE FEEL OF A BIG HOLLYWOOD MOVIE."

where the 21st Century technology comes in – they can hide stuff and add layers of things, but basically it's all in camera, which is phenomenal.

There's a kinetic feel to even the "talky" sequences – what techniques did you use?
J.J.'s approach to covering a sequence is that the camera is never still. It's always moving. That tool of kineticism gives a subliminal feel of anxiety. The perception is that the camera, which is a character all the time, has life to it. The viewer is vicariously picking up those movements – which are all organic – and therefore feels the trepidation or whatever you're trying to transmit.

Is that technique something specific to J.J.?
The way J.J. does it is specific to him. Other directors try to do it and don't really go 100 per cent and allow it to happen, but J.J. from the beginning will commit to something and let it go. That's what he did: he committed to the look and feel of the movie, which has kineticism to it plus an awful amount of camera flares and aberrations that occur throughout in real time, in order to degrade the image and give it a more organic feel. We did that at the time.

Did that ever feel "wrong" when you were doing it?
I was brought up in the camera department, which has a very disciplined bunch of rules. You're encouraged never to break them. But all J.J. wants to do is break the rules, so sometimes your instinct is to say this is completely wrong, but you do it anyway, and when you see it, his judgment call was completely right.

What was the biggest challenge for you?
To maintain the quality level that I tried to start out with, which was to give it the integrity that J.J. was demanding for this movie. *Star Trek* had to have integrity: it needed the weight, the ballast and the feel of a big Hollywood movie. It required a huge amount of help from all the different departments and technicians – just keeping that all focused was a very difficult thing to do. The hardest thing for me was to maintain that all the way through.

What did you think when you first saw it?
The first time I saw a cut of the film, I was the only person there who hadn't seen it, and all the editors and producers asked me an incredible number of questions. I could not answer them, because I had been watching it as a viewer – it sucked me in the first couple of seconds and spat me out at the end. I wasn't aware of what had happened, I was so engrossed in the story. This movie is so "up". It really is great. ◢

"[The] tool of kineticism gives a subliminal feeling of anxiety"

Taking the
captain's chair

SPOCK

ZACHARY QUINTO

Main photos © Zade Rosenthal

Always keen to expand his horizons, Zachary Quinto has diversified into TV roles and movie production in the intervening years between *Trek* movies, but what new challenges face Spock in *Star Trek Into Darkness*? The former *Heroes* star talks to Tara Bennett.

Star Trek Magazine: Even before *Star Trek* came into your life, you had exposure to a passionate genre fandom when you played Sylar on *Heroes*. Has your association with *Star Trek* made your life terribly different?

Zachary Quinto: My life has changed in the last few years just because of the increased exposure my work has generated. I did *Heroes* and *Star Trek*, but that's more to do with celebrity than the genre of it. I feel like my life is mine still, which is always my primary goal.

You had a long span between these two films to go off and do other things. Did you appreciate getting some space away from such a huge franchise and iconic character?

I was grateful for the space and time between the two movies, on a lot of levels, for building a company to produce movies and working on other sets, for sure. I feel like it's a part of building a career that is rooted on a foundation of diversity and diversifying, and doing other stuff besides just sci-fi or horror. But I also love the world, and love the people that come together to create it, so I'm also grateful to come back to it.

"I FEEL LIKE I GOT TO CONNECT TO THE PHYSICALITY OF THE CHARACTER IN A MUCH BIGGER WAY THE SECOND TIME AROUND."

Spock hunts down the enemy
in *Star Trek Into Darkness*

CAREER NOTES

TELEVISION
24 (2003)
So NoTORIous (2006)
Heroes (2006-10)
American Horror Story (2011-13)

FILMS (AS A PRODUCER)
Hostage: A Love Story (2009)
Margin Call (2011)
Dog Eat Dog: A Short Tale (2011)

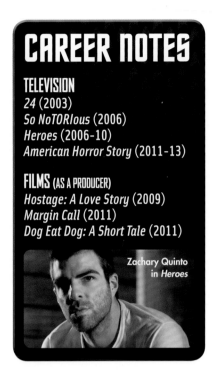

Zachary Quinto
in *Heroes*

Unlike the rest of the *Trek* cast, you had the unique experience of Leonard Nimoy portraying his version of Mr. Spock right alongside yours in the first film. Did you feel yourself aligning your performance to his initially?
I didn't feel in any way influenced by Leonard, other than by his friendship, and by the conversations he had with me about the character. I feel like J.J. was so specific, and the entire film, the first time around, was built around the idea of us reimagining these characters, and bringing them to life in our own way. I felt that was my job, and my mandate that I was working with. I didn't feel

> "THE ENTIRE FILM, THE FIRST TIME AROUND, WAS BUILT AROUND THE IDEA OF US REIMAGINING THESE CHARACTERS, AND BRINGING THEM TO LIFE IN OUR OWN WAY."

like having Leonard participating in the film or in my proximity was in any way distracting.

Mr. Nimoy has spoken so highly of you as a person, and about what you did with the character. How has your relationship evolved as friends and actors?
My relationship with Leonard is rooted in mutual appreciation and respect. I feel like my friendship with him, outside of the context of the film, is just about us as human beings and not about the character that we both inhabited, and that he created so indelibly in the original series. I think it's also just a part of knowing him, and witnessing

Spock and Harrison's thrilling fight
sequence in *Star Trek Into Darkness*

Spock and Kirk on the Bridge

the man that he is, and knowing the life he has lived has been so connected to the franchise, and to the character. He's worked in wonderful ways to diversify his creative experience since the original series and the films. I adore his energy, because he's so incredible, but I don't really ever relate him to my job anymore. That was early on when we first started, and before I formed my own relationship with the character. But now I feel like my relationship with Spock is about my own experience, and about the story that I am telling, and that's where I've gone with this film.

What first jumped off the page for you when you read the script for *Star Trek Into Darkness*?
Well, it was very clear to me from the beginning that it was a bigger story, there was more at stake, and there was more action. You could tell from the get-go it was just bigger. Also, when we made the first movie, there was a writers' strike, so we didn't have the opportunity to collaborate with Bob, Alex, Damon, and J.J. the first time around. In the second film it was great, because the script really changed in the weeks leading up to the shoot. We worked on it, talked about it, and rehearsed it, so things came out of that process that we weren't able to the first time, so that was exciting.

Your Spock seems to be less focused on just the logical side of his being. What is he wrestling with as a character?
Yes, it's less about the logic, though the logic is always there, and the logic rules the way the character relates to any situation or other people. But for me, it's about not being so settled in that

one point of view but pulled in a couple of different directions, in terms of emotional life, integrity, and also passion, which I think is a big part of him. I think in the first film, the character had less control over all those disparate elements. I think in the second film he understands them more, but chooses when to engage different versions of himself in order to accomplish the tasks he needs to do, and to save lives.

Is Spock in a very cerebral place in this sequel?
No, in general with Spock, I have a lot more action in this film. There are some huge sequences that

Spock in command

he is a part of, that were really exciting and challenging for me. It was great for me to step into a more active role, and not be so cerebral. I feel like I got to connect to the physicality of the character in a much bigger way the second time around, and that excited me a great deal. I dove into training for a couple months before shooting.

What types of sequences were you training for?
I did a lot of wire work. I did a lot of sprinting in the film. It was a lot of different stuff, so I trained in general ways and then with a stunt trainer. It was really fun. This movie has

Zachary Quinto as Mr. Spock

everybody in different situations and scenarios, on their own, in a way that the first movie didn't. We're all scattered and spread out in different places, yet all working together. We're not such a unified front, and we have to break into factions to get things done.

Where are Spock and Kirk as peers at the film's start? Is the First Officer getting along with his Captain?
It's a little bit roundabout in that Spock begins as an adviser, and then evolves into a first responder. He witnesses things and makes observations, and stands behind Kirk trying to guide him to make good decisions. Sometimes Kirk does, and sometimes Kirk doesn't, but when he doesn't Spock is right there to do whatever he needs to do to help the situation.

How are they pushing one another forward as Starfleet officers and as burgeoning leaders in this film?
They help each other grow, and learn lessons, and face things they need to face in order to be better at their jobs, and be better in the world. The first film was a lot about Spock's journey and Kirk's journey individually, and how they arrive to the place where the missions began. This one is really about each of them learning, primarily, a distilled lesson that will only help them as crewmates, and as friends moving forward in their lives. There's a great threat, and they do confront some serious situations together.

John Harrison is a daunting foe in this story for Kirk, but what does he represent to Spock?
Harrison represents a lot to Spock. He represents uncertainty. He represents a threat and an adversary. He also represents a teacher, in a way, because everyone learns lessons from Harrison. He's a formidable opponent in a lot of ways, and everybody has to stop in order to make sure he is defeated.

Would you say Spock also has more invested with this threat in the wake of Vulcan's destruction? When Harrison hits London and San Francisco in this film, is Spock more motivated because he's still mourning another recent, devastating loss?

> **IF YOU COULD SWIPE ANY PIECE OF *TREK* TECH FOR YOUR REAL LIFE, WHAT WOULD IT BE?**
>
> I guess it would be to be transported; the whole Transporter set-up.

Spock to the rescue

"EVERYONE LEARNS LESSONS FROM HARRISON. HE'S A FORMIDABLE OPPONENT IN A LOT OF WAYS, AND EVERYBODY HAS TO STOP IN ORDER TO MAKE SURE HE IS DEFEATED."

Sure, I think he's definitely doing anything he has to do to prevent that kind of destruction and casualty ever again. I think there's something very personal about that for Spock in this film, that carries over for sure the echoes of the loss of his mother, the people who were very close to him, but also a significant portion of his race. I think he's got a fierce protectiveness in him in this film, and a fierce determination to make sure he prevents that kind catastrophe from ever happening again, anywhere in the galaxy.

Is Spock's relationship with Lt. Uhura as prevalent as in the first film?

It's definitely an undercurrent of the story, the relationship between Uhura and Spock. I wouldn't say it's a primary plot point for either character this time around. It's sort of sustained in a way that it can be revisited in future installments, if we do future stories. In this film, there are more pressing issues, but there is an undercurrent. They do both resolve things in their relationship with each other that I think would be satisfying for those looking for that.

With so many existing and new characters in the film, did the story dynamics allow you to work with some of the cast that maybe you didn't work with much in the first film?
I felt like it was a little bit in the opposite, because I didn't get to work this time around with people I enjoyed [last time]. I didn't get to spend much time with Simon Pegg, or even with Chris Pine (Kirk) this time. We split off for a big chunk of the film, and go off and try to help each other from a distance. But what I lost with the familiar, I gained in working with Benedict, which was significant. We got along really well, and I liked working with him. And with the gang, we do spend a fair amount of time together for the big set pieces. ⏶

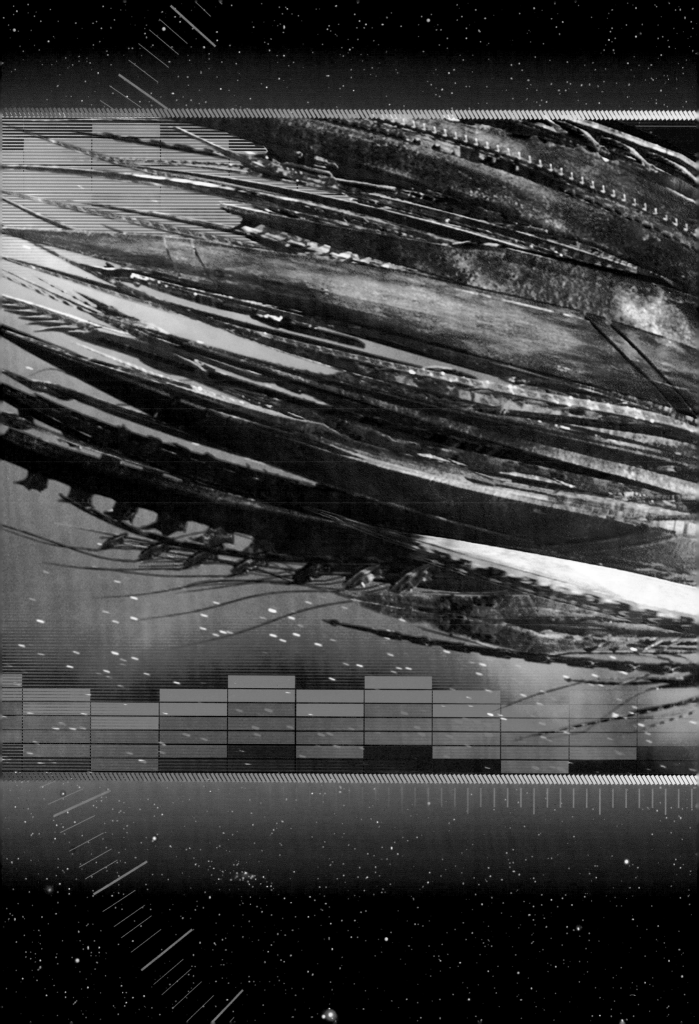

BEN BURTT
SOUND DESIGNER

It might be the most high-tech *U.S.S. Enterprise* that we've yet encountered on *Star Trek*, but the sounds accompanying it were made using many of the same techniques that went into the creation of the show back in the 1960s, one of the many ways that sound designer Ben Burtt paid homage to the

A tour of the engine room

How did you get involved with this incarnation of Star Trek?

I got a call last October from one of the Paramount executives, Marty Cohen. I've worked for him before, and he asked if I would be interested in coming down and looking at the movie in its current stage and giving them some opinions about the sound. I went to a screening, and at that point, they were completing a mix of the movie.

I was brought in to consult, and after my first meeting with J.J., and hearing what they had done so far, the film wasn't really completed. They weren't entirely happy with where they were at with the sound, and they needed some new input. I work for Pixar, but I had a lot of vacation weeks coming to me, so I took my vacation and worked on *Star Trek* for the next six weeks. I really had a great time.

Essentially my task was to design sounds, starting with what we thought were the most important things in the movie and working down the list in the time available. We were trying to give a distinctive identity to every spaceship's engines and everything about the *Enterprise* – different rooms and different functions for the equipment – and create sounds for the weapons, the *Narada* and the imploding planets. I had to work specifically on certain areas of the movie that really needed some deep thought, particularly the first few minutes: how to get into the film with sounds and music. The space jump, the arrival at Vulcan in the asteroid field, and of course the entire ending of the movie with the shoot out in the *Narada* and the supernovas were other sequences I had to focus on.

It was unusual for me because usually when I've had the privilege of working on a film, I've worked on sound design much earlier in the process, starting in preproduction and through production. It was interesting to do something as huge as *Star Trek* in such a short time.

But I was well prepared for it – I love *Star Trek*. I was a big fan of the original TV show. Back when it began, in 1966, I was just going off to college in North West Pennsylvania, where you couldn't get television reception. But my father tape recorded the shows off the television, sent me the tapes and I would listen to *Star Trek* in my dorm bedroom with headphones on.

My acquaintance with the original show was through sound, which was so good, it brought to mind such clear imagery as to what was going on. By the time I got to see the show, I felt I knew everything about it – I understood the ship, the transporter and the phasers. I really admired the sound in that show and a few years later, when I started working on *Star Wars*, I was inspired to take what I liked about *Star Trek* and dial it into my approach toward *Star Wars*. That material was iconographic – you identified it with the credibility and the depth of *Star Trek*.

Listening out for classic sounds aboard the *Kelvin*

"I HAD TO WORK SPECIFICALLY ON CERTAIN AREAS OF THE MOVIE THAT REALLY NEEDED SOME DEEP THOUGHT, PARTICULARLY THE FIRST FEW MINUTES: HOW TO GET INTO THE FILM WITH SOUNDS AND MUSIC."

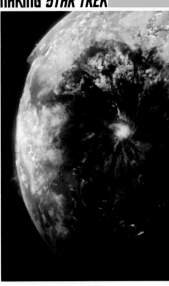

"All ahead, warp factor 5."

"I WANTED TO GO BACK TO THAT ORIGINAL TIME PERIOD, FOR FUN, AND MAKE SOUND EFFECTS THAT WERE IN THE STYLE OF THE ORIGINAL SHOW AND USE MANY OF THE SAME TECHNIQUES."

The mantra on the film seems to have been that the makers were honoring what came before but not slavishly following it – whereas the sound seems closer to the original...

When I decided on a game plan for my contribution to the film, I felt two things were lacking in what I had heard thus far. Firstly, it didn't really sound like a science fiction movie to me: the sound effects seemed very contemporary and Earthbound. There wasn't something about them that made me think "I'm in space." In my opinion, there was a lack of identity, a lack of a feeling it was addressing the legacy of science fiction.

Secondly, what I felt we wanted to do, where we could, was touch base with what we loved about the sound in the original series. It didn't work to take the library from the original series – which we could have done – and start cutting it in. We wanted to honor it, and I felt there was a real value in making that connection. Here was a chance to do with sound what J.J. had done with the rest of the movie. Just as with the uniforms, or the *Enterprise* itself, the design was similar enough that you said, "I feel comfortable with this because it does connect with the original nature of the series."

I wanted to go back to that original time period,

for fun, and make sound effects that were in the style of the original show and use many of the same techniques. I felt that if I did that, the result would in some way feel like the original without being exactly the same. It was my interpretation of what I liked about the original library of sound in that show.

Two things in the original *Star Trek* effects were revolutionary: Roddenberry had his team create lots of detail. Every room in the ship sounded different. Every button made a noise, when you pressed a lever or a switch. Not only were there sounds articulating all these things to make them sound like they were real, but they were very musical sounds. Somebody pressed a button, there was a little melody. That was not in the movie at the point I came on: you'd just hear a little beep. If it was *Star Trek*, it needed to sing a little bit and feel like it was alive. You really felt there was a complex operation going on and it was fun to listen to. The ships and the weapons and the ambiences of the places they went to were a form of music. When they went to planets there was always a tone going on, like a ringing bell, or chimes in echo. I tried to create sounds in that style.

The other thing that was used a lot in the original show was shortwave radio recordings and sounds off of transmissions and Morse code, things you can

BEN BURTT

Best known for the creation of the signature audio effects in the *Star Wars* films for Lucasfilm (including Darth Vader's breathing, the "voices" of R2-D2 and Chewbacca, and the lightsaber sounds), four-time Oscar-winning sound designer and sound editor Benjamin Burtt, Jr. is also the recipient of honors from the British Academy of Film and Television Arts, as well as numerous other societies recognizing achievement in motion picture sound production.

Apart from the six *Star Wars* movies, Burtt's sound work appears in the *Clone Wars* television series as well as 10 different *Star Wars* video games. He worked on the four *Indiana Jones* movies, *E.T.*, *Munich*, and *WALL-E* (where he also voiced the title character) before joining J.J. Abrams' *Star Trek*.

Burtt scripted four episodes of the *Star Wars* animated series *Droids* (on which he was a story editor); the documentary *Niagara: Miracles, Myths and Magic*, and *The Adventures of Young Indiana Jones: Attack of the Hawkmen* (which he also directed). His other directorial credits include the IMAX movies *Destiny in Space*, *Blue Planet*, and *Special Effects: Anything Can Happen*.

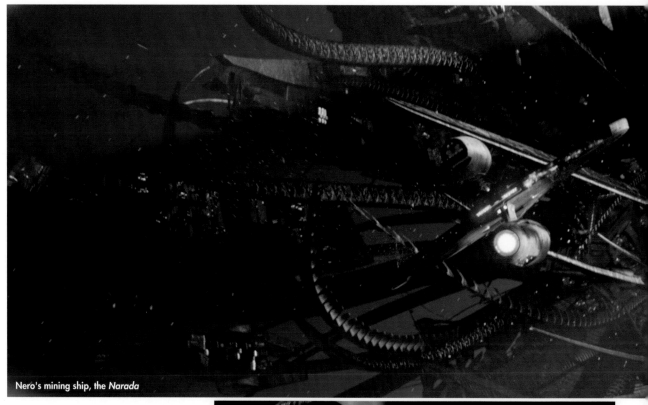

Nero's mining ship, the *Narada*

pick up in-between the dials on a shortwave radio. I love that sort of thing and I've collected it for years. There's some of that in the original *Star Trek* television show – and the whole beginning of the movie, that first minute or two where the *Kelvin* is coming into view, is all short wave radio sounds. It reads to the audience that you're way the heck out at the edge of the universe, barely in contact. Things are far away: there's these disembodied sounds that are being transmitted back and forth. That's not the way the sound was, but I wanted to make it seem like the ships were way out there. They're supposed to be encountering something new so I tried to capitalize on this legacy in science fiction of using radio.

MOOG MUSIC

How did you recreate the button sounds?
A lot of the original sounds in the *Enterprise* back then were generated by a very early primitive synthesizer, so I borrowed an old Minimoog, and I have an old ARP. Activating the transporter, the tones in the hallways of the *Enterprise,* some of the Bridge sounds, and quite a bit of the button pressing and activating sounds were done with the Moog. Some were radio transmission sounds that I had edited together.

There are different stories as to how the squeaky doors on the *Enterprise* were created originally, but I remade the sound by squeaking my tennis shoes on the floor of the kitchen in a little water, and added a little tire pump. The doors on the new ship were a little more complicated: they didn't just open one sliding

door, so I would stick that sound in, and then there were a few other little motor sounds that the other editors put in to articulate the rest of the function. I was happy with just the squeak! It's a similar sound but not quite the same.

The phasers are visually nearer *Star Wars* blasters in this version...
Yeah, like a tracer bullet rather than a beam. They had made a couple of phaser sounds that were already on the track, but I went back and made new ones. Of course I couldn't use a steady beaming sound like the original, but I made most of the new sounds by taking a long spring, that is stretched out about 30 feet long, which I have suspended from a very tall ladder. Essentially, when you tap a long wire – and a spring is a long wire compressed into a smaller space – the sound travels along that wire, but the high frequencies travel faster than the low frequencies. If you tap it at

Phasers set to stun.

> # "I MADE THE *NARADA* ALWAYS HAVE A BIG SHRIEKY SCREAM WHEN YOU SAW IT, CREATED PARTLY OUT OF A SYNTHESIZER SCREAM I MADE, AND A WHALE."

just "bang bang bang," but "be-bang, bing, BONG..." It makes it much more interesting to the ear. They had some great metal pings of things ricocheting around, and I put some gunshots underneath to give it a little more weight.

Were the background sounds for the *Kelvin* and the *Enterprise* designed to reflect the difference in time between them?

All the tones on the Bridge of the *Kelvin* up to the point where the *Narada* comes out of the black hole were pretty much created using shortwave radio sounds. Supervising Sound Editor Mark Stoeckinger added some alarms for the *Narada* coming out the black hole. The bed for the Bridge is actually the same bed that I used for the *Enterprise* but for the *Enterprise* I added

new things on top of it. There was a sense that they were connected in some way, but the *Enterprise* had additional new technology.

OLD IS NEW
How did the process work?

I would sit there and first play the movie in my little mix room. I put on the wall my *Star Trek* Fan Club certificate from 1970 signed by Gene Roddenberry and I wanted to go back and escape into that world. When I would put sounds in, I would try to feel as if I were there. I would put little things in that would excite me – I wouldn't try to imitate directly but I was trying to be inspired by what I liked about the original show. If I had a choice, I would try to make an interpretation of what they did back then – so it felt like it was what you heard back then but now you can hear the detail. There weren't that many quiet moments in the movie where you could hear small details, but there were a few. We tried to get as much character in as possible.

I made the *Narada* always have a big shrieky scream when you saw it, created partly out of a synthesizer scream I made, and a whale. It had an oceanic look to it, like a squid, so every time you cut to that it had a distinctive accent to it.

The *Jellyfish* had this counter-rotating fuselage, so I made a sound that had a tremolo but a variation of speed such that it sounded like it was spinning. I took the sound of some NASCAR racers going round a corner howling on their tires and made it into a cyclical tremolo, similar to what I did for the Podracers in *The Phantom Menace*. That was dictated by the function of

one end, it's a clicking sound. At the way far end of the spring, the high frequencies get there first, and then the mids and then the lows – it's like a Doppler shift. That's what was used for the original photon torpedoes in the TV series, which goes back to the 1953 *War of the Worlds* and some of the Paramount comedy films from the late 1940s: it's in the Bob Hope/Hedy Lamarr movie *My Favorite Spy* and in some of the Jerry Lewis movies. I made a similar type of sound – higher-pitched, shorter and sharper – for the hand phasers.

There are variations of it, different lengths, and in some the pitch goes up rather than down. To make a gunfight work, like the one on the *Narada* at the end, you have to have each shot be a little bit different so once again there's a sense of musical orchestration, not

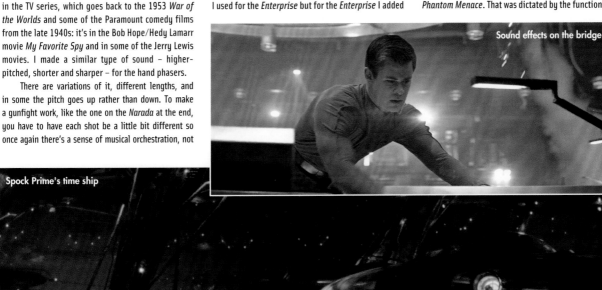

Sound effects on the bridge

Spock Prime's time ship

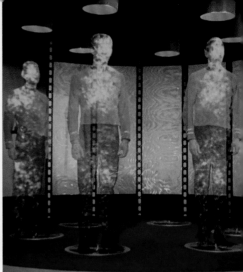

New sounds for the *Enterprise*

"I MADE SOUNDS FOR THE NEW MOVIE THAT HAD A FUN FEELING TO THEM, THAT TRIGGERED A SENSE OF REWARD FOR LISTENING TO THEM."

the ship: it was spinning and it was a contrast to the heavy music going on in most of its scenes.

In the original show, the *Enterprise*'s engine sounds were created using a test oscillator, a sound generator that creates a tone to line up recording equipment. They ran that through a bit of a plate reverb chamber, so you could turn the sound from a low frequency to a high frequency – and that's what you heard in the Bridge as the *Enterprise* increased speed. I went back and got an oscillator from a college I went to back in the 1960s and an old reverb chamber, connected it all up, and redid the effect. I gave it a lot of variations because the *Enterprise* moves at different speeds and does a few different things in this new film, but I wanted to base it on that original idea that the *Enterprise* wasn't just a roaring bass – it had a tonality to it.

A lot of the musicality of the sounds came about originally because Alexander Courage did a music session during the pilot of the original series where a whole gang of musicians created sounds for many of the things used in the series. They did a library of interesting tones and things that became the transporters and parts of the *Enterprise*. Because it was done by musicians and with a musical sensitivity, I think it's one of the things that made *Star Trek* so pleasant to listen to.

With music, you get an immediate emotional response from the audience. You tap into how we listen to music. The show was very musical and the effects were in a major scale – it was upbeat and had an optimistic feel. In the intervening shows, often the transporter and other sounds were in a minor key or discordant, so were not fun to listen to. It didn't give you that same feeling of optimism. I made sounds for the new movie that had a fun feeling to them, that triggered a sense of reward for listening to them. Being musical and positive at the same time had an innocence. Perhaps it was a good thing to go back and try to recapture the innocence of another time.

How did you find working with the film's composer, Michael Giacchino?
We've worked together on Pixar movies and he was excellent in the sense of discussing what to do, to make a relationship between music and sound effects. He was much more open to thinking of the soundtrack of the movie as including all things – dialogue, music and effects. A lot of the time you work with composers who only hear their music and although the music is wonderfully important, you need to make everything work in concert. The sound effects have to orchestrate in some way with the music. Most often, the music can't be changed so you have to change the sounds to

be something that works with the music – that takes a lot of experimentation. In science fiction you have some latitude because you're not necessarily trying to keep sounds as people expect them to be. No matter what sounds you've made, to make it articulate to the audience and ultimately more dramatic, you have to make them work with the music somehow. That is a major effort. Most films don't allow time for that to happen.

J.J. was driven by the music. When there were decisions to be made, often the music would "hit the accelerator pedal," whereas quite often I felt there were times where that wasn't the thing to do – but then you get into the subjective realm of taste. I think the music comes out better if you're careful when you use it. *Star Trek* is a film that could easily go over the top because it's got so much density of visual action. One of the things I tried to do was to thin things out, to try to find any opportunity to let things be quieter, and let sound effects and music fall into the background for a while so you're just thinking about the dialogue, and save your energy for the right moments.

Overall, did you enjoy working on *Star Trek*?
J.J. gave me a license to do just about anything. I would do it, present it to him and he would decide what he wanted and didn't want. That was a fun experience. Having not a lot of time was good in some ways because it forced me to operate on instinct. I have a love for the original show and this was a great opportunity to take whatever I've learned and apply it to *Star Trek* and be part of that experience. I tried to pretend it was 1966 and do it as best I could. I wanted this film to connect with what I loved about the original show. I hoped it would succeed subconsciously for fans who would sense that emotional connection, so they would feel comfortable and secure. And for people who didn't know *Star Trek*, it would use the same values from the original show and capture them again. ▲

FEELING THE HEAT!

Special effects expert William Aldridge has raised the temperature of many Hollywood film sets, thanks to his proficiency in pyrotechnic wizardry. His most recent challenge? Blowing up Starfleet.
By Calum Waddell

Remember those formative years in school, before the puberty-led perils of adolescence, when the teacher would ask what each child's mother and father did for a living? Well, one thing's for certain – the offspring of special effects co-ordinator William Aldridge can give one of the most eye-opening replies imaginable: '*My dad blows stuff up*.' Indeed, Aldridge is renowned in Hollywood for his skills as a pyrotechnician, as well as for his abilities in miniature and practical effects work. The master of mayhem made his debut in all things *Enterprise*-related with 2009's *Star Trek* and recently contributed to *Into Darkness* – although Aldridge's resumé stretches back to the 1970s, taking in the likes of *The Goonies* (1985), *Die Hard* (1988) and the aptly-titled *Demolition Man* (1993).

Star Trek Magazine: How did you first get into the effects business?
William Aldridge: My career began way back in 1973, shortly after I got out of the military. My dad was in the grip department (the technicians responsible for lighting and rigging on a film set) at Universal, and I went down there and enquired about employment. It was a case of being in the right place at the right time, because I got a job as a carpenter, there and then. That lasted for just two weeks but, luckily, I got a call-back to do some night work at the studio. Then, one evening, someone walked in and asked if anybody in the carpentry department could make models. I raised my hand and they took me on. I actually knew nothing about it, but I went in on the Monday morning and began doing miniatures for a movie called *Earthquake*. I seemed to do well at that and decided to pursue effects. Then it was one show after another, and it all went from there.

You've worked with high-profile directors, from Luc Besson on *The Fifth Element* (1997) to Michael Bay on *Pearl Harbor* (2001). How does J.J. Abrams compare?

The first *Star Trek* was a lot of fun to work on. I was on the first unit team, working with J.J. Abrams the whole way through. I can tell you that he is a great guy, a really smart producer, director and writer, but also a very nice, energetic and warm personality. He is also incredibly dedicated to *Star Trek*. On the first film, and also on *Into Darkness*, he was working for 18 hours a day. Someone would often have to come up to him and say 'Okay J.J., that's it – we need to wrap for the day or else we won't get turnaround for tomorrow.' I swear, he would work 24 hours a day if you'd let him (*laughs*).

You're known as "Bill Effects" in the industry, mainly for your pyrotechnic skills. Of all the effects you created for *Into Darkness*, what sticks in your mind most?

For this sequel, we built these really nice spark machines. They were very cool. There's a great sequence in *Into Darkness* that's set on a volcanic planet. As with everything J.J. does, he wanted this to look as realistic as possible, and he wanted a good mix of practical and CG effects. So we had a lot of fire, and a lot of fireballs, shooting 30 feet up into the sky (*laughs*). We also built a spark machine which expelled this coconut charcoal. We put that in these little air movers and propelled it through jets of fire, so it would look like volcanic ash and substance. It was crazy to see all of that shooting around the set but, man, it looked incredible. There is something very rewarding about going to work and creating a 30-foot fireball (*laughs*).

Working with such dangerous elements on set, how much of your work is preparation to prevent accidents?

I love the sequence in the new sequel where this enemy craft comes in and starts shooting at all of these people. But the bullet hits are not like normal bullet hits. This is nothing like a western – these are bullets which melt stuff and disintegrate things. It was a very busy set-up, because there had to be a lot of people running all over the place. Five of the actors were stunt-people, and there were also a few members of the principal cast, while the rest were extras. It was mayhem (*laughs*). So we had to plan for that. It can be especially tricky when there are explosions going off. No matter how small the explosion is going to be, there is always danger. The threat of someone getting hit in the eye with a piece of flying debris cannot be taken lightly, and I need to make sure that doesn't happen. Everything has to be very carefully mapped out and planned ahead.

It might surprise audiences to know just how much of your work *doesn't* involve big bangs.

There were a lot of little things that we had to work on for *Into Darkness* that you wouldn't even think were special effects. For instance, we had 15 elevators in the ships that all had to do different things. And all of the doors had to be different from one another on the *Enterprise*. The production designer asked for that. A lot of the things we do are the pneumatics, so you can push a button and the door will open nice and smoothly as a character walks in and out. The shuttles had to have little clamshell doors too. All of that stuff is mechanical, and it needs a lot of preparation. There were also a lot of little explosions on *Into Darkness*, but it wasn't a big

Star Trek Into Darkness
director J.J. Abrams

Kirk keeps us hanging in suspense

The attack on Starfleet Command

> "THE DAY IS SURE TO ARRIVE WHEN THE TECHNOLOGY WILL SIMPLY SCAN THE ACTORS AND THEN CREATE THE WHOLE FILM AROUND THEM."
> WILLIAM ALDRIDGE

pyrotechnic show. We started out shooting at the famous Dodgers Stadium in Los Angeles, where we had to organize a snow scene. However, in the end, we took up half of the parking lot with snow, and there was no easy or quick way of tidying all of that up when we called cut. It was a major clean-up job just to get everything back to normal again, believe me (*laughs*).

How does *Into Darkness* measure up against the 2009 movie?
I think the new film is even better than the first. The script is terrific – probably one of the best sci-fi stories I have ever read. With the last movie, J.J. took a lot of time to establish everything. It was important to present the classic *Star Trek* characters to a new audience, and to explain how and why they became the way they are, whilst also paying respect to that vast legacy of Gene Roddenberry. But with *Into Darkness*, because J.J. has established all of that great back-story, we just get into the meat of the whole thing.

With Abrams' dedication to ensuring no *Into Darkness* spoilers slipped into the public consciousness before the movie's release, is it true that *Into Darkness* began production under a top-secret name?
[J.J.] does not want anyone to know about what he has planned. He really wants to creep up and surprise the *Star Trek* audience. I remember that the first *Star Trek* script went under the title *Corporate Headquarters*. Then *Into Darkness* came to us under the pseudonym *HH Project*. We were instructed not to write *Star Trek* on anything. Even a little note on the script had to refer to *HH Project*. We shot *Into Darkness* at what used to be the space allotted to the Howard Hughes Aircraft Company, so that is how the title *HH Project* came about.

CGI seems to be taking over so many elements of movie effects work. Do you see much of a future for practical effects artists?
The day is sure to arrive when the technology will simply scan the actors and then create the whole film around them. Everything will be generated on a computer. A lot of the kids nowadays are only playing videogames, and that's maybe why stuff like *Transformers* is such a hit. Some of those films look a little like videogames to me. My sons go and see all that stuff, and they love it, and that is the young audience that the Hollywood executives want to reach out to. Now, if you were to ask me, I think practical effects generally look better. A lot of the time we work with the computer guys to combine elements of animated effects and the real thing, like you see on the two *Star Trek* movies. I work very well with the visual effects people, and I respect them a lot.

Khan keeps us hanging in suspense

There have been some great achievements in your long career, but an Oscar has eluded you so far. Will 2013 be your year?
I would love if my other new movie, *Lone Survivor*, got nominated [for an Oscar] in the same year as *Into Darkness*. Then the Academy decides it is a tie! That would be the dream, right? I remember that *Die Hard* was nominated for its effects, but *Roger Rabbit* beat us, which was, of course, a disappointment. It always seems that every time something I have worked on gets nominated for its effects work, another great show comes along and beats us out. With the first *Star Trek* it was *Avatar*, which had been 15 years in the making. That was always going to be a hard one to go up against (*laughs*). What can I say? I've had a great run. And who wouldn't want to be working with J.J. Abrams on one of the biggest films in the world? I'm a lucky guy! ⋀

ERIC BANA IS NERO

Eric Bana's career has seen him Hulk out, battle in the Trojan Wars, and lord it over an English Tudor court. But his role as the time-traveling Nero, last survivor of Romulus, gave him some very different opportunities...

Nero's anger

"Fire!"

Although the primary focus of Roberto Orci and Alex Kurtzman's script for *Star Trek* was the coming together of the Bridge crew of the *U.S.S. Enterprise*, it was abundantly clear to everyone involved with the movie that someone with great screen presence would be needed to play the part of their first adversary. As casting director April Webster noted, "Kirk and these guys had to cut their teeth on the strongest guy possible. We discussed a lot of different names, and from the beginning Eric Bana was one of the top names."

For Bana, the call for *Star Trek* came during a sabbatical from acting, after filming his role in *The Time Traveler's Wife*. However, he recalls that he was "a little skeptical" when he first heard about plans to revive *Star Trek*. "I wasn't sure how they could do it," he admits freely.

However, once he became aware that J.J. Abrams was at the helm, Bana's skepticism diminished. The Australian actor had gotten to know the director "a little over the years through a mutual contact," he explains. "We'd discussed working together and striking up a working relationship. When I knew that J.J. was attached and that it was a prequel, that got me interested, and then I read the script – and I was immediately in love."

To Bana, "the script was incredibly smart, well written and well structured. I was actually quite blown away by it, to be honest. I thought Roberto and Alex had done an unbelievable job of paying enough service to many characters so succinctly but thoroughly. It was a real triumph of screenwriting: I was quite shocked. Whenever you read something that is that good for so many different characters, you're just bamboozled as to how they've managed to do it."

And the villain himself was intriguing. "I felt like there was enough complexity to Nero to get me interested," Bana notes. "I said to J.J. that the script was such a thrill ride from start to finish, and Nero was such a wonderfully mad and entertaining villain, that I just had to get involved. After that conversation with J.J., I was on board."

Although he wouldn't describe himself as a Trekkie, Bana "was very aware of *Star Trek*. The original TV series was pretty big when I was a kid. It was probably the only TV show that my brother and I didn't get into a fight over! I loved the original series. I hadn't seen any of the films, but the original series and the characters from that were my reference point."

Writers Orci and Kurtzman have noted that their successive iterations of the movie script beefed up the character of Nero, but for Bana, many of the ingredients were in place from the start. "Essentially, I was trying to draw on an incredibly tragic and brutal past," he says. "For me, that was the most important thing about him. I felt like Nero had this incredibly tragic back-story, and had become a villain as a result of the things that had happened to him. That was more interesting than just him being born as the villain. To me, he was just a Romulan who had had a lot of amazingly treacherous things done to him, so whilst he wasn't human, I felt there was some sort of characteristics there that humans could definitely relate to, and I wanted to draw on that."

Bana agrees that the days have gone when audiences will accept two-dimensional bad guys. "I always like it when we have a reason to know why our villain is the villain, and not just have to accept that he's the villain because we're told that he is."

However, that initial reading did flag up one potential problem. "I guess the only concern I had initially was that I identified the fact that *Star Trek* was

> ## "THE SCRIPT WAS INCREDIBLY SMART, WELL WRITTEN AND WELL STRUCTURED. I WAS ACTUALLY QUITE BLOWN AWAY BY IT, TO BE HONEST."

A starship as spiky as its captain

Face to face with an angry Romulan

definitely a 'heroes' movie' not a 'villains' movie,' and the danger would have been to not have given enough to Nero," he says. "But J.J., Roberto and Alex were already attentive to that, so that really came along and was being really well serviced by them. They gave me enough to play with!"

One element really attracted Bana. "I was fascinated by the notion of Nero being in jail on Rura Penthe for so many years, him biding his time, and being unbelievably patient in enacting his vengeance," Bana says, adding, "Some of that is not played out in the film, because it's not in the final cut, but it'll be out on the DVD. I think there's nothing scarier than a patient villain. He can be very patient and Zen-like. He's mastered the idea that revenge is a dish best served cold!"

However once Spock Prime has arrived back in the 23rd Century, everything ramps up. "I think when it all starts to happen, it all starts to happen very quickly for Nero," Bana continues. "I think he does end up in a state of pure, uncalculated rage. That was fun to play because to play a cool, calculating villain all the way through would not have been so much fun."

Nero's defiance as the *Narada* is drawn into the singularity also pleased Bana. "I really loved the way the character is treated at the end of the film," he enthuses. "That was a big draw for me. At the end he was given a choice, and he chooses to just stay aboard his ship and die with his own honor. I thought that was very, very sad – and very, very cool."

LOOKING THE PART

By the time that Bana was preparing to start filming, "90 per cent" of Nero's distinctive look had already been sorted out. "I played a bit with the pattern of the tattoos with Neville Page, our designer. We experimented with various different ways of laying out the pattern until we got it right," he recalls. "You had to be careful because a lot of the time, a pattern that looked great on the paper, or even in the flesh, didn't work on screen, because suddenly it resembled a symbol that you wouldn't have thought of when you initially looked at it. Or from three-quarter side on, it was a boat anchor or something else! We had to be very

ERIC BANA

An Australian by birth, Eric Banadinoviç is the son of a Croatian logistics manager and a German hairdresser. He was raised in Melbourne and showed a flair for comedy as a youth, but it wasn't until he saw *Mad Max* that he realized he wanted to be an actor. Still, he didn't believe it an attainable goal and worked as a bartender until he was encouraged to try stand-up comedy. Bana began at the Castle Hotel and soon after hit the local circuit. It wasn't until 1993 that he gained wider exposure by appearing on Steve Vizard's *Tonight Live*. This led to regular work on the sketch comedy series, *Full Frontal*. After four years, he went on to star in *The Eric Bana Show*, receiving a Logie Award for Most Popular Comedy Personality.

Bana made his film debut in the drama *The Castle* which led to the indie hit *Chopper*, where he used his mimicry skills to portray the psychopath Mark Brandon "Chopper" Read. His work earned him the Australian Film Institute Award for Best Actor. He featured in Ridley Scott's *Black Hawk Down* and gained international attention as Bruce Banner in Ang Lee's *Hulk*. More action roles followed with Wolfgang Petersen's *Troy* and Steven Spielberg's *Munich*. More recently, he played King Henry VIII in *The Other Boleyn Girl*, and took another leap into the fourth dimension in *The Time Traveler's Wife*.

Recommended performance:
Avner: *Munich*

Eric Bana as Nero

"NERO DOES END UP IN A STATE OF PURE, UNCALCULATED RAGE. TO PLAY A COOL, CALCULATING VILLAIN ALL THE WAY THROUGH WOULD NOT HAVE BEEN SO MUCH FUN."

careful because things move very quickly in pre-production when you're coming up to your first day of shooting. We had to make sure that we had it right, and we wouldn't get a month into dailies and have to go, 'Let's take a straw poll – can anyone see the lady and the mermaid pattern on the top of his head?'!"

Bana also ensured that if he was going to be in the prosthetics for long shooting days, they were as comfortable as they could be under the circumstances. "The prosthetics only underwent very minor changes, just for comfort and actability," he explains. "Sometimes you make a really tiny change with the prosthetic, or the glue, or where it's attached, and it can really make a difference to your ability to convey expression. We had a few goes at that in pre-production to get that right." Indeed, by the time they were a week into shooting, Bana notes that "he began to look completely normal to me,

You wouldn't like him when he's angry...

and regular humans started to look weird!"

And while *Star Trek Magazine* can attest to the fact that on set the Romulans with their bald heads covered in tattoos were distinctly intimidating, Bana laughs that his family are used to seeing him looking unusual. Even his bald look didn't faze them. "I've done it three or four times now for films," he says. "They love me fat, skinny, bald, hairy – they're used to it. This is a crazy job!"

Bana points out that while he gets his share of fights within the movie, fans should look out for more. "There's a fair bit that's not in the film as well," he says. "There's a couple of fight scenes that I'm sure will be on the DVD."

Unlike some of the other cast members, Bana wasn't trained in a specific mode of fighting. "Nero was quite brutal in his fighting style – it wasn't overly specific for my character," he says. "It was more Chris Pine, who had to be on the receiving end. I've done fight scenes with a number of actors, but Chris is so tough and fast and hard; he's one tough customer and it made for an epic encounter."

And his biggest challenge looking back on the *Star Trek* experience? Bana reckons it was "just finding Nero's physicality. I had to come up with a physicality for the character that was believable and not too ridiculous." ▲

HEART
OF DARKNESS

You have to be a heavyweight in stature and delivery to trump the Klingons as the biggest badass in a *Star Trek* film, but actor Peter Weller did just that in *Star Trek Into Darkness* with his intense portrayal of Starfleet zealot Admiral Alexander Marcus.
By Tara Bennett

A true believer in the necessity of might and firepower to neutralize the impending threat of a Klingon war, Admiral Marcus' path to peace may be the antithesis of Starfleet's exploration mandate, but he does make a remarkably clear case that gives one pause as he barks out his personal ideology. It takes a strong actor to make that kind of big antagonist real and far from caricature, which is why J.J. Abrams convinced Peter Weller to bring his incredibly persuasive persona into the rebooted *Trek* fold.

The duo met in 2010 when Abrams enlisted Weller to guest star on *Fringe*, where he played a scientist tampering with time in the seminal episode, "White Tulip." Two years later, Abrams came knocking again asking Weller to take on the heavy lifting of Admiral Marcus, the man whom Kirk would have to face down in the final act of the film.

A PhD student, actor, and television director, Weller already had plenty on his plate when he was approached, but the actor says he couldn't resist working with the director again. *Star Trek Into Darkness* also represented the actor's second foray into the universe, as he had done a two-episode stint on *Star Trek: Enterprise* as John Frederick Paxton, another zealot with similar thematic ties to Marcus.

As Weller helped promote the DVD/Blu-ray release of *Star Trek Into Darkness*, we had an exclusive chat with the actor about the fun of working in the *Trek* realm, his defense of Marcus' convictions, and his other creative endeavors.

STM: In 2005, you appeared in two episodes of *Enterprise*, "Terra Prime" and "Demons." Did you ever intend to return to the franchise, or was *Star Trek Into Darkness* a surprise?

No. I gotta tell you, I did [*Enterprise*] as an homage to Leonard Nimoy. Leonard is one of the oldest acquaintances I have in the business. The third job I ever did was a play with Leonard, so we're old friends. Manny Coto, who was writing for *Star Trek: Enterprise*, convinced me to do it. Manny is very seductive and an old friend too. He said, "You have to do this homage to Leonard." I was not really ever a Trekkie. I watched the original series as a kid; I watched some of it, but I didn't know all the ins and outs. For all of the science fiction that I have been part of, I admire science fiction for its invention and its alternate realities but I'm not a science fiction guy. I'm an Art History/Roman History guy. So I was conned into that and I had a great time. Whether or not *Star Trek* was going to come back [into my life], I have to tell you, I didn't care. But when it was resurrected brilliantly by J.J., I marveled that this thing is never going to go away. This thing is in perpetuity.

STM: Was there a moment that really clarified the scope of *Trek* to you personally?
Nothing showed it more to me than when I was directing *Longmire*, a wonderful series for A&E, and I got the day off to present about 45 minutes of my dissertation in front of about 150 art professors and it was also the same day as the *Star Trek Into Darkness* premiere. So there I am doing the art academic thing and this limo comes to pick me up to go to the premiere. We are coming down the street and I see *thousands* and *thousands* of people. Now listen, I've been nominated for an Oscar, an Independent Spirit Award and SAG award, so I've done the red carpet, but I'd never seen *anything* like this. The Paramount representative said, "It's a cult. It's never going away." There were people older than me and younger than me and it really hit me. *Star Trek* is forever, so there you go. You heard it here first. [*Laughs*]

STM: And that's certainly a good thing in our book.
It is good. It has a moral theme in it, which all great science fiction has. It has a social, political and moral theme of how to treat people.

STM: Switching topics to characters with more of a hawk-like point of view, your character Admiral Marcus is a man who really represents the antithesis of what Starfleet is supposed to be about.
[*Laughs*] I *do* want to defend Marcus. He is saying I want to sacrifice these guys, but everything Marcus says is true. The war with the Klingons is coming. We do need special weapons. Marcus did wake up Khan in order to use him, and he did admit his mistake. So everything Marcus said is right, it's just too bad he was going to sacrifice the well-being of the *Enterprise*. But yeah, there is a morality to Marcus too.

STM: Do you have to believe everything a character like Marcus spouts to play him, because you are completely authentic with his message on screen.
You have to agree with everything he says. You read it and you get it. The only character that truly doesn't have a point of view is Iago in *Othello*. He says in the end when asked why

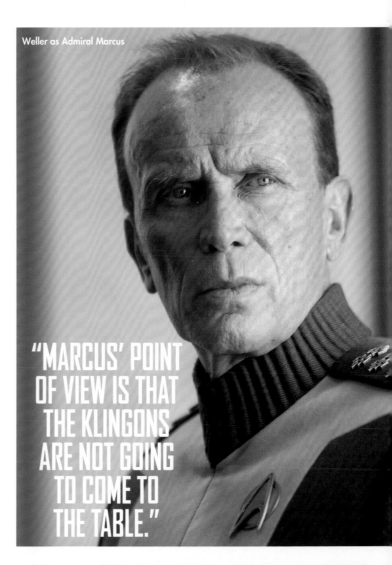

Weller as Admiral Marcus

"MARCUS' POINT OF VIEW IS THAT THE KLINGONS ARE NOT GOING TO COME TO THE TABLE."

NOT A SCI-FI GUY?

In a long and varied career, Peter Weller has notched up a fair number of science fiction and fantasy credits:

The Adventures of Buckaroo Banzai Across the 8th Dimension (1984)
A madcap sci-fi comedy adventure starring Weller as unorthodox genius (and rock musician) Doctor Buckaroo Banzai.

RoboCop & RoboCop 2 (1987 & 1990)
Paul Verhoeven's bloody and insanely satirical thriller starred Weller as cybernetically enhanced cop Alex Murphy. The actor handed in his badge after the first sequel.

Screamers (1995)
Cult adaptation of Philip K. Dick's dystopian short story "Second Variety," which sees Weller as Colonel Joseph A. Hendricksson fighting his way through alien enemy lines.

Odyssey 5 (2002-2003)
Manny Coto's TV series about a group of astronauts who survive the destruction of Earth, then go back in time to try to prevent it. Weller portrayed space shuttle commander Chuck Taggart.

Batman: The Dark Knight Returns (2012)
Frank Miller's seminal comic book saga brought to life in animated form, with Weller donning the Caped Crusader's cowl.

did you do this, "My lips are forever sealed," so you don't know why he does it. Jealousy? But everybody else has a point of view, and Marcus has a very strong point of view, so it's very easy to tap into that, even if it's not my point of view. Look, Marcus' point of view is that the Klingons are not going to come to the table. They're not going to handle things with grace; they're not graceful people. Osama bin Laden was not a graceful guy and you were never going to get that guy to sit down and negotiate, so that's substitution there. What they say in the Method is substitution is a personal invention or personal replacement of what the script says that you can't really do. I've never been a General, but I have been a leader. I've never been in a spaceship, but I have been in an airplane. I've never been to war, but I've been in a bar fight when I was a kid, so there you go!

STM: Marcus is in a position of being a father figure for Pike. But I wonder if you thought Marcus also saw himself as a better father figure to Kirk, especially after Pike's demise?
I felt like a father figure for Pike. I guess Marcus felt fatherly towards Kirk up to a point. When Kirk lets loose and stops believing him, then no. It's a really hard call and really good writing for Marcus.

STM: One of the most interesting twists for Marcus was his relationship with his daughter, Carol Marcus. Do you feel it humanized him and gave you something to work with in terms of the audience's sympathies?
Yeah, I think the most magnificent thing they did for Marcus was put the daughter in,

because he had something to lose – family. It heightens the stakes for Marcus and makes it personal when she is on the *Enterprise*. It's great stuff that he's ready to blow off a whole set of circumstances and people on a ship, but then his daughter is on the ship and confronts him. It's great stuff! To give an antagonist that many facets of life is wonderful.

STM: At age 66, you are busier than ever in so many different arenas. Are you enjoying playing in several different sandboxes, or do you find yourself leaning in one direction more than others?
Everything changes, but I love the balance I have now. I have a two-year-old son and a wonderful wife. I have to finish this PhD. She said to me, "Finish that damn PhD, because I'm sick of it," so I am. I am probably teaching a course on directing actors for film at UCLA. I might teach another class about Hollywood and the Roman Empire. They accepted the one course and are now reviewing the other course. It's a way of being of service. I like that, giving back, which is satisfying. I also love directing. I'm going to go off and direct Guillermo del Toro's new show, *The Strain*. I have a very rich life. I don't ever intend to retire. I intend to be in the movies until I'm 102 doing something... or looking at the Mediterranean going peacefully on to the other land. So yeah, it's a combination of the PhD, acting, teaching and directing remarkable shows like *Sons of Anarchy*, *Longmire* and now returning to Roberto Orci's *Hawaii 5-0* again. I love directing for television. There's a time limit, a drive to it, an immediacy and a patience, if you will, to it that is really rewarding. I can't complain. I have a great life! ⋀

Alice Eve as Carol Marcus

Peter Weller hits the red carpet

JOHN HARRISON/
KHAN
BENEDICT CUMBERBATCH

s © Zade Rosenthal

...ng made his name as Conan Doyle's super sleuth,
...lock, Benedict Cumberbatch has gained a legion of
...playing the good guy. That all changed when the
...atile British actor took on a villainous role in *Star
...Into Darkness*, as the mysterious John Harrison
...Khaaaan!)...

By Christopher Cooper

Trek Magazine: When you first got the part
...John Harrison, how did they entice you to
...Did you get to read any of the script, did
...audition, or did they come after you?

Cumberbatch: J.J. pitched the idea of the
...to me before I did a taped audition on my
...my friend's kitchen. I was just enjoying

Christmas, and getting these frantic calls from
the USA saying 'can't we get your tape?' There
were literally no casting agents in town, so I was
scrambling about, trying to make something
work, thinking this is not going to happen before
Christmas. Then my friends came through, very
last minute, saying 'we'll tape you, it's fine'.

"TERRORISM IS A DAILY PART OF OUR NEWS CYCLE, A DAILY PART OF OUR LIVES THAT WE'VE ALL BEEN AFFECTED BY IN SOME WAY."

CAREER NOTES

THEATER
Hedda Gabler (2005)
Frankenstein (2011)

RADIO
Cabin Pressure (2008)
Neverwhere (2013)

TELEVISION
Cambridge Spies (2003)
Sherlock (2010)
Parade's End (2013)

FILMS
Hawking (2004)
Atonement (2007)
Four Lions (2010)
Tinker, Tailor, Soldier, Spy (2011)
War Horse (2011)
The Fifth Estate (2013)

Harrison has a point to make

they really wanted to help out, so we did two takes of, I think, two or three scenes, picked the best ones, and then it took a whole day to compress the file. I'd never sent something via weshare or transfer or dotcom or whatever, some Russian website, so that was another day of faffing about.

I was eager to find out, after all that effort, then I got word that J.J. had gone on holiday, so I kind of forgot about it, as much as I could. I got the call on the evening of New Year's Day, and it was amazing. I didn't fully know what I was getting involved with, I hadn't read a whole script, so I took a leap of faith based on the pedigree of J.J.'s film making, and obviously the first rebooted *Star Trek* in 2009, which I loved.

Were you a *Star Trek* fan prior to being cast?
I never really saw it that much. I've just never had a fanboy following of anything in particular – I'm sure I'm missing out, whether that be football or *Star Trek* – so I've managed to avoid being an all out fan. This is the first proper involvement I've had with anything of this ilk, so I did a little bit of catching up on what kind of universe I was stepping into, but the primary lure was to work with J.J. and the cast of the first film, who I thought were outstanding. I realized as I was watching it that I must have let a little bit more Trekkie folklore creep into my mind than I'd thought, because I got a massive kick, as I think a lot of fans did, of seeing this genesis, this origin story, of seeing Uhura, Scotty, Spock, all of them, coming together for the first time with Kirk. I remember in the cinema – having literally been told by everybody I know, not only *Star Trek* fans, that it was just a really good film – being moved to tears for the first five minutes, then laughing out loud for the next ten, and being utterly on the edge of my seat for the whole ride. I thought it was brilliant.

J.J.'s interpretation impressed you enough to sign up for the sequel?
Really that's the only calling card I needed. I mean, the guy's very smart, he does things with great integrity, and there's a huge well of good feeling behind what he does. It is about family, and he's created this family of slightly strange – as they were in the original series – this daring mixture of all sorts of people. In a very revolutionary way, the original TV series held a light up to a possible Utopian future of ethnic cooperation, where people will be able to mix, no matter what race, species, color and creed they were.

Can Spock's logic defeat Harrison?

Harrison gets arrested
for his terrorist attrocities

What I remember about the TV series is the idea that each one of them seems to be a morality play that taught us more about the now, even though the metaphor was the future. For procedural television, they were extraordinarily imaginative in the creation of these other worlds, creatures, and languages. I can completely understand the fascination of the fans in this rich universe of intelligence and information. I must've been hit a little bit by that when I was younger, but I didn't really take it in until I saw his film. I thought 'Yeah, I really care about these people,' and that's what J.J. is brilliant at doing. I love his film-making, and sure enough the man in person is all about family. Any character development, any concerns you have, anybody who is additional to the cast or the crew of the *Enterprise*, you care about them all, they all have a case, and it's very beautifully crafted, so you have a proper, character-driven drama that happens to have all the lure and excitement of *Star Trek* added with the amazing possibilities of modern film-making. It's just thrilling work to do, it really is, because you know you're doing a big film but based on a very detailed, good script, with good ideas.

You've joined this cast, this family, but you've joined as the bad guy. Was that a difficult experience?
They were so respectful of that. There were only a couple of moments, which you'll probably get when you see the film, where it's very much about me being outside of their world, or

"I TOOK A LEAP OF FAITH BASED ON THE PEDIGREE OF J.J.'S FILM MAKING."

separated in some way in what I'm doing. The joy of the character is that he does come from within, so there's an awful lot to play with there, in the context of who trusts who, who wants what from whom, and how to get what you want from whoever that might be.

There was only one occasion where I had the discipline to pull away from their camaraderie, and sit away in a corner and brood, darkly, because I had too much fun with them. I had so much fun with them, I hope that doesn't reflect itself in the film, because otherwise I'll be useless (*laughs*).

They're a lovely, incredibly witty, brilliant bunch. That's a great thrill, to meet people at the top of their game, who've already established themselves in such a strong franchise. To work with them was just a real kick. A real kick.

I think Chris [Pine] is one of the best leading men there is. He's extraordinary in the performance he gives. He's really smart, he varies his game, he's constantly grinding away at the script, the story arcs. He's always paying attention to where his character is, and Kirk's story in the overall scheme of things. A great guy to hang out with. And Zach [Quinto] really is

one of the most bizarre human beings on the planet, a very special person. Zoe Saldana is a breath of fresh air, beautiful but so funny. [Simon] Pegg is already a proven entertainer. John Cho and Karl Urban are, again, hysterical. Bruce [Greenwood], what a lovely man he is. We had so much fun hanging out together in LA, it was genuinely a really joyous experience. I spent all my time just laughing.

Did that good humor extend to the set, and working with J.J.?
J.J. I think has actually now done some improv. He's done some stand-up, he's that good. He dared himself to do it, like he does with everything he turns his hand to. He's not a dilettante, that man, he's a polymath. He really is an expert at anything he turns his hand to. He'd doodle a cartoon, and then turn it into a 3D printable graphic, he'd come up with an idea for Nickelodeon – this is just in the breaks between set-ups, with the IMAX being changed over. He'd beatbox, he'd play music that was comically fitting for the moment of the day. He's irrepressible as a force of creativity, and a lovely human being to work for.

Your character in the movie seems equally charismatic though rather less wholesome. He's coming at things from a certain perspective, a different world view, isn't he?
I think playing any outsider is always intriguing. To me, it's always about the ambiguity, that's

Cumberbatch as Khan

what interests me. We're trying to reflect certain aspects of the times that we're in. Terrorism is a daily part of our news cycle, a daily part of our lives that we've all been affected by in some way. The ambiguity I was talking about is the idea that these are people who are, from their perspective, the underdogs. They're the people who are fighting against superpowers, in this case they are the people who are fighting against what they see as tyrannical dictatorships masquerading as democracy. There's an awful lot of, I think, quite soulful purpose behind what people do, it's just how they do it is where I depart on any empathy.

To play a character, you have to obviously go to a place where destruction and mayhem is attractive, it's his way of getting what he wants. I [as Khan] cause an awful lot of destruction, and I'm kind of squeamish – I can't watch myself and go 'Yeah, cool!', I kinda go, 'Oh my God, how many people perished in that explosion?!' It worries me (*laughs*). When I have my children and introduce them to what I do, I don't want them to be looking at my back catalogue of good work and watch me kill loads of people.

"THERE WAS ONLY ONE OCCASION WHERE I HAD THE DISCIPLINE TO PULL AWAY FROM THEIR CAMARADERIE, AND SIT AWAY IN A CORNER AND BROOD, DARKLY."

Kirk faces his deadliest enemy in *Star Trek Into Darkness*

It was a very interesting thing to mine this feeling of utter disenfranchised exclusion from a political process, which in this case is taking over the universe that my character inhabits, and rebelling against that. Without giving too much away, there's a big purpose to why he does what he does. I hope that the audience can stop going 'boo, hiss' and listen for a second, and go, 'Well, you know, he kinda has a point.' Before going 'boo, hiss' again.

It's also a very physical role.
I had some serious set pieces in this film, which were great fun to train up for, and he's a very strong, capable warrior, so I had to pick up the pace very, very quickly. I had a training ritual. I went up about four suit sizes in the space of month, ate a lot of protein and worked out a lot to do that, and was training for these

choreographed fight sequences, stunts, wire work, and all sorts of fun and games. And some of that was caught really early on, by some paparazzi, when we were filming the fight that Spock and I have. That was the first shot anyone got of either of us on the second film.

Talking of leaked photos, and the level of interest in your character specifically, has it been hard keeping spoilers under wraps?
I have to be so guarded with what I tell you. There's so much I can't tell you, and I wouldn't want to. I do buy into this whole process. I genuinely got a kick out of seeing *Super 8* not having been spoon-fed the whole plot through spoilers in trailers. I'm not trying to be some nurse or nanny here, fans' appetites are fans' appetites, and I'm not the person to dictate who eats what and when. All I try to express is

that my personal preference, as a filmgoer, means that I'm quite loyal to this process of letting people come to the film with a little bit of undiscovered anticipation, and discover things in the moment of viewing.

I think it's going to be really thrilling. I can't wait to see it. I think I'm as eager as any fan of the first film is to see how it all comes together. It's going to be a real treat.

And all off the back of an audition recorded on a mobile phone...
I completely fell on my feet, and all by chance. I mean, this iPhone audition could have gone very wrong. I wasn't as focused as I should have been, because of Christmas, you know. I took it all very lightly, I guess. Maybe that's a lesson in life, to take things lightly, and then good things come of it.

TURNING TO THE DARK SIDE

Creating the strange new worlds and dangerous environments for *Star Trek Into Darkness* was a thrilling yet demanding experience, as Production Designer Scott Chambliss explains.
Interview by Bryan Cairns

As Production Designer on *Star Trek Into Darkness*, Scott Chambliss is the master of his surroundings. For *Star Trek* (2009), he transformed a Sony sound-stage – two massive hangars which once housed Howard Hughes' Spruce Goose – into alien landscapes, a drinking hangout for Starfleet Academy types, and of course the *piece-de-resistance* – the starship *Enterprise* herself. But as thrilled as Chambliss was to be returning for his second consecutive *Star Trek*, the ambitious *Into Darkness* proved much more demanding than his earlier outing.

"Our story is a darker story," says Chambliss. "It's also bigger, and our themes of good versus evil are subverted a little bit because you don't really know who the good and bad guys are. It's not clear-cut at all. In terms of my job on the previous movie, I had three distinctly different cultures that were present in that story. This time around, our story is not about a bunch of different cultures around the universe, dealing with each other. It's about Starfleet itself, and the mysteries of Starfleet that become revealed unhappily along the way."

Part of Chambliss' responsibility is to help establish a signature look for the film. As the title infers, *Into Darkness*' palette is, well, much darker than other *Trek* adventures.

"There's Gene Roddenberry's fundamentally optimistic point of view on the world and life that we've tried to adhere to," explains Chambliss. "Going into darker and more complicated storytelling, we could potentially lose sight of that. The task of showing the dark side basically meant there still had to be a recognizable foundation of elements of the light side of this coin. My metaphor was taking

> "OUR STORY IS NOT ABOUT A BUNCH OF DIFFERENT CULTURES AROUND THE UNIVERSE, DEALING WITH EACH OTHER. IT'S ABOUT STARFLEET ITSELF."

The Qo'noS set was inspired by the sun installation at the Tate Modern, London

Starfleet HQ at red alert

Chambliss tinkered with the Bridge set for *Into Darkness*

something beautiful, like the *Enterprise*, and militarizing it to the hilt. What would that look like, and how would it feel when you were inside?"

NEW WORLDS

Despite a resumé containing such high profile blockbusters as *Salt* and *Cowboys & Aliens*, it's Chambliss' history with J.J. Abrams that stands out. They've collaborated on the Abrams-created TV series *Felicity* and *Alias*, as well as the Abrams-directed features *Mission: Impossible III*, *Star Trek* (2009) and its sequel. By now, the two have established a successful rhythm when tackling a script, which means Chambliss knew exactly which items needed to be immediately addressed.

"I would say the most time-consuming, in terms of beginning the conceptual approach to what we finally agreed on, and finally built, were these two different planets, Qo'noS and Nibiru," reports Chambliss. "Because they are new worlds we are trying to define, they took a lot of attention and a lot of negotiating, both creatively and financially. Because we wanted both worlds to be really huge in scale, and get as much in camera as we possibly could, we went through all sorts of processes."

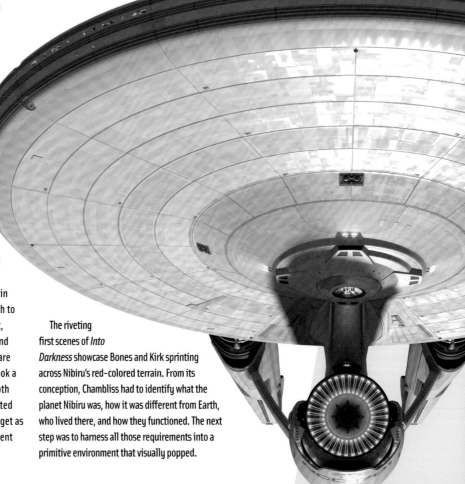

The riveting first scenes of *Into Darkness* showcase Bones and Kirk sprinting across Nibiru's red-colored terrain. From its conception, Chambliss had to identify what the planet Nibiru was, how it was different from Earth, who lived there, and how they functioned. The next step was to harness all those requirements into a primitive environment that visually popped.

Harrison looks out onto a toxic Qo'noS

The chase sequence on Qo'noS

"At first, Qo'noS was going to be a super-industrialized place, where the off-product of their industry was so toxic, they basically turned the planet itself into an utter waste zone," reveals Chambliss. "In doing that, they altered the environment so much it became a non-stop storming planet. There was only lightning, storms, and crazy wind in the sky. You couldn't even walk the surface of the planet, because it was all oceans of toxicity. They had burrowed down into the planet and built their city on top. They kept building higher and higher because the meth level got higher and higher.

"When it came down to dealing with it, the sequence wasn't fully fleshed out in the beginning, which is normal," continues Chambliss. "We came to a place where it was pretty clear what was going to be happening here was a big action sequence. There wasn't a whole lot of dialogue or a whole lot of story content. It was just going to be action. Ultimately, that took us to a place of trying all different kinds of environmental pieces of this overall picture of toxified Qo'noS. We ultimately landed in what was probably a factory. It could have been a munitions factory. It could have been a place for building spacecraft. But long ago, something really dreadful happened there, and it was basically like a Chernobyl at this point. That's what you see in the film.

"I think I did 14 different versions of the set," he adds. "Each one had a different specificity of what it was, and why it was the way it was. Nothing really landed with J.J. It finally got to the point where I needed to do something a lot more abstract. In the trailer, you see this big, glowing, lensy thing in the background, the big halo behind them. That was inspired by one of my favorite artists, who does these epic scale installations. His name is Olafur Eliasson. He's the guy who did this gigantic sunshine at the Tate Modern (the renowned museum of modern art in London). That was the thing I kept staring at, and seeing the scale of a human being in front of it, and thought, 'This is so cool. Maybe this is a way into what we're doing, playing with a massive sunburst or light source, or whatever the hell it was going to be, against our villain, who is supposed to be the baddest guy on Earth.' But the epic scale of that glow even makes this huge bad guy look tiny."

"The population is kind of aboriginal," says Chambliss. "They haven't developed into a complex or technical culture at all. They are based on their own religion at this point in their evolution. The guys had written it as a beautiful island, and it sounded like Fiji or somewhere like that, quite gorgeous and lush. The one thing that I immediately didn't want to do was go to some place that looked like a great vacation spot and shoot this. So what are tropical environments other than green? They are lush and green, green, green, green. I thought, 'Let's flip that and go red, red, red, red. Let all the vegetation be red.' That was inspired by one of my favorite plants I see in Hawaii, which is a kind of bamboo. Its trunk tends to have large sections of this really vibrant fuchsia. It's so otherworldly. I just started with an assistant messing around in Photoshop, messing around with bamboo forests and inverting the colors so that they become this lush ruby red. In flipping some of the other tones around, they became this mossy golden color. Suddenly, it felt like a tropical world, but was utterly different than what we've seen."

TOXIC SHOCK

Another key set was the Klingon homeworld, Qo'noS. Faithful *Trek* followers know the alien race to be savage warriors, and Chambliss wanted to capture that hardened, ruthless spirit.

UNDER LOCK AND KEY

Details surrounding actor Benedict Cumberbatch's new super-baddie, John Harrison, have been scarce. Who he is, and his intentions, remain a

"I TINKERED WITH EVERYTHING, BECAUSE IN THE FIRST ONE I DID, I DIDN'T GET TO FINISH EVERYTHING."

mystery. Nonetheless, there is some buzz-worthy released footage that finds Harrison securely locked away in a clean, sleek, metallic brig, with a glass window almost taking up one wall.

"There were going to be two sequences in the brig and, initially, the guys wanted a Hannibal Lecter moment," reports Chambliss. "It was going to be a series of small, single prison cells on a radius. It was going to be a mixed circular space with all these cells. It was supposed to feel huge. The key element of how that thing functions is you see the big black eyeball in the back of the cell with him. That's supposed to be their surveillance system, and you can see versions of that all over the larger brig set. That was based on a really cool, ball-shaped Italian television from the 1970's. In terms of why it's big and open and glassed like that, it's so everything could be seen from all the angles, at all times. It's very clear there's no means of getting in or out, once you're in there. You have to be released by some means, which we ended up not showing. There was going to be a portal that opened up in the glass, for someone to be taken in or out of."

And then there's the *Enterprise*. Chambliss already had the opportunity to put his own mark on the legendary starship, in the previous installment. Once production wrapped, instead of destroying the elaborate piece and having to start again from scratch, it was simply broken down and segments were stored away. For *Into Darkness*, those sections were polished off, rebuilt, and fine-tuned.

"They saved the Bridge, the Med Bay, and the Transporter Room," says. "We pulled all of

The red, red, red planet Nibiru

Kirk and Bones are chased by the natives

those out of mothballs, and some of it had disintegrated over time. I think they trotted the Bridge out for a couple of commercials, and one whole section of it fell off a truck, literally. We were able to put everything together, and refreshed a whole lot of it. We got to add some

"THE GUYS WANTED A HANNIBAL LECTER MOMENT."

new sets as well. We have a turbo plaza, which is an oval, connective hub, leading from different hallways that go to different sets.

We had a whole scene in Kirk's quarters. We designed this kick-ass set – I so want to do it if we do another *Star Trek* movie. It was a beautiful set, and says some really cool things about who Kirk is and what his priorities are. Unfortunately, we couldn't afford that.

"I tinkered with everything, because in the first one I did, I didn't get to finish everything to the state of perfection I wanted it to be, or at least what I thought would be perfect," concludes Chambliss. "For the Med Bay, we extended it tremendously. In the transporter bay, we changed the effect of the glass pieces that ring that bay. I wasn't terribly happy how it looked on film in the original one. Then in the Bridge, there are glass navigational panels behind the crew members, who are standing at their little consoles, to the left and right of the captain's chair. I pulled my original design for them, which we were unable to complete the first time around, and actually completed them. They have a more substantial presence and a better look to them. We do have an amazing new set in the *Enterprise*. It's based on a location that has never been shot for film before. It adds a physical scope and a huge amount of detail, in a really impressive space, that will add so much big-picture value to this movie. I'm really pleased we shot in that. I basically had to lie down on J.J.'s office floor until he agreed to look at it with me, let alone shoot it." ∧

The *Enterprise* brig set in which Harrison is held captive

An Enterprise
corridor at red alert

BRUCE ALMIGHTY

Interview by Tara Bennett

As Admiral Christopher Pike, Bruce Greenwood took a classic *Star Trek* character into an alternate timeline and gave him a new spin – as a father figure to Jim Kirk. Yet despite Pike's on-screen death in *Star Trek Into Darkness*, he reveals an unwillingness to give up the character quite yet.

Star Trek Magazine: You aren't known for doing a lot of science fiction films, so *Star Trek* must be quite a unique experience for you?
Bruce Greenwood: I haven't done a lot of genre pictures, and then J.J. called and invited me to come play on *Star Trek*. I've done a few science fiction things. When I think back, I've been working so long you tend to forget what you've done. Other people look at your list of stuff and tend to say, "Oh, I see a trend here." You only do two or three things a year, so you look back at 25 years of work and go, "Oh, well I guess there is a trend." It evolved so slowly I didn't really notice it.

As a young kid in Canada, was *Star Trek* something you watched?
The original series was on my radar as a kid because everybody liked seeing the women in the tight costumes. I was very young... early adolescent, so I was transfixed. I didn't realize back then that the themes were essentially classical themes. I don't think I appreciated it that much, frankly! (*Laughs*)

You must have been aware of the fanbase, and their legendary dedication?
I had no idea, until I was well into the saddle, that expectations were very high and I would never know as much about the *Trek* world as virtually every member of the audience that came to see it.

Did you feel pressure to jump in and research the previous series and films?
Once you get a sense of how much people cared about this world, and the history of the world and the lore of the world, you go and do the research anyway. You realize people are so invested in it that you want to find out why.

Since there are almost 50 years of *Star Trek* to catch up on, was this the most research-intensive role you've done?
It was up there in terms of the homework. I think I probably did more scholastic homework on *13 Days*, because there was so much time-specific material to get through during the period that movie represented. With *Star Trek*, it mostly involved watching lots and lots of episodes. Everybody on the set – [Damon] Lindelof, Alex [Kurtzman] and Roberto [Orci] – are deep files on the subject, if you ever, ever had a question. They even had a few people who were even more completely into it, and they were on the set at all times.

The Admiral gives Kirk (Chris Pine) a stern talking-to (*Star Trek Into Darkness*)

> ## "CHRISTOPHER PIKE IS A CAREER GUY WHO BELIEVES DEEPLY IN THE RESPONSIBILITY OF STARFLEET AND THE POTENTIAL TO DO GOOD."

Actor Jeffrey Hunter portrayed Captain Christopher Pike in the original *Star Trek* pilot "The Cage." Did you feel any connection between his Pike and yours?
They are almost opposites, because Jeffrey Hunter's Pike was so ambivalent about staying with Starfleet. He was so torn, and that's not the case with Admiral Christopher Pike at all. Admiral Christopher Pike is a career guy who believes deeply in the responsibility of Starfleet and the potential to do good, and to observe the Prime Directive when it's not. Yet you can look at it as though they are two sides of the same coin, because of the parallel universe.

Did you feel a need to infuse any of Hunter's performance style into your character, as a subtle nod to fans?
Although he is well known to real fans of the series, he's not nearly as known as Shatner and Nimoy. I know Chris [Pine] was judicious with his tip of the hat to Shatner's mannerisms, and the same with Zach [Quinto]. But I wasn't sure if it would really be apparent to anybody if I was to try and salt Christopher with Jeffrey Hunter's Pike.

We did get your Pike in a wheelchair after he was

PIKE'S PROGRESS

"The Cage"

In the original *Trek* timeline, Pike captained the *Enterprise* for over 11 years before relinquishing command to Jim Kirk. Promoted to Commodore and serving as Fleet Captain aboard a Starfleet training vessel, Pike was mortally wounded in a tragic accident which left him confined to a life-supporting wheelchair. Spock would risk his life and career to help his stricken former commanding officer, diverting the *Enterprise* to Talos IV where the ex-captain could enjoy what remained of his life in full health (a very real illusion created by the telepathic Talosians).

Pike's progress in the alternate timeline – created after the incursion of Nero and the destruction of the *U.S.S. Kelvin* – took a rather different path. Convinced to join Starfleet by Alexander Marcus, and presumably after a respectable career in space, Pike is spending his days recruiting potential officers for training at Starfleet Academy. Perhaps his decision to enter academia was prompted by the same events on Rigel VII that caused Pike to question his career choices back in the original timeline?

Unfortunately for Kirk's mentor, there was to be no Talosian reprieve in this universe. While he would survive a violent encounter with Nero, just a few years later Khan's thirst for vengeance would result in the Admiral's untimely death.

tortured by Nero, which is an allusion to TV Pike. It was the one obvious tip of the hat!

You've done every kind of film, from low-budget indie to blockbusters. Is it especially impressive

to work on films of *Star Trek*'s scale?
It's awe-inspiring. You walk into these massive, massive sets that people have taken hundreds of thousands of hours to design and create, and you can't help but be exhilarated and cowed at

Pike (Greenwood) offers more words of
wisdom to the wayward Kirk (Chris Pine)

the same time. It's one of those times when you walk in and go, "Wow, people have just given their absolute all to create this environment." When the environment is such a critical element of the whole experience, you know people are going to be investing as much creativity as they can muster. It's inspiring, energizing and fills you with respect.

We don't get a lot of history about your Admiral Christopher Pike. Did you spend much time thinking about it?
In terms of back-story, you are free to create infinite memories, points of view and attitudes you think

Bruce Greenwood as Christopher Pike

AUTHORITY FIGURE

Star Trek's Admiral Christopher Pike isn't Greenwood's only commanding role. If a casting director is looking for a multi-faceted performer with genuine gravitas, an effortless on-screen presence and easy-going charm, they need look no further than Bruce Greenwood – as his resumé attests:

GRAVITAS
"Thirteen Days" (2000) & "National Treasure: Book of Secrets" (2007)
You need weight to convince as a U.S. President, let alone as the ill-fated John F. Kennedy. Greenwood features as the iconic President in docudrama "Thirteen Days", and as a fictional President in the "National Treasure" sequel, alongside Hollywood heavyweights Jon Voight, Helen Mirren, and Harvey Keitel.

PRESENCE
"Batman: Under the Red Hood" 2010
If you need a costumed hero who can steal a scene just by standing in the shadows, then Batman is your go-to guy. Greenwood iced the cake, lending his vocal tones to both Batman and alter-ego Bruce Wayne, in this animated adaptation of DC Comics' "A Death in the Family" and "Under the Hood".

CHARM
"Summer Dreams: The Story of The Beach Boys" 1990
While this TV movie may have been a warts-and-all dramatization of the family travails of pop legends Brain and Dennis Wilson, the laid-back summer grooves of The Beach Boys and Bruce Greenwood (who played Dennis) are a perfect match.

the character has that you and you alone invent. For example, look at the scene between Chris and I in the last film, where I am haranguing [Kirk] for making the wrong decision. I see what's written and intended, but then wonder what if I took a completely different tack where I'm gentle with him and choose not to tell him his ship is being taken away? I play that scene out in my head. And then what if I focus more on Spock and pillory Spock for not coming through sooner? So you go through a different series of choices in a confrontation, so when you are actually doing a scene all that stuff goes through your mind, and you choose in that instant to say what happens in the script. The options are always there, so you don't feel as though you have to say a certain thing. You make a choice in the moment how to say what is written.

Pike really is a surrogate father to Kirk, and your on-screen rapport with Chris is so real. Was the rapport really that natural?
The reality of that relationship for me is, to a large degree, that I am really, really fortunate that I am tremendously fond of Chris. He is a wonderful, wonderful guy. Sometimes you have to create out of whole cloth and sometimes it's just there. With Chris, you don't have to work hard to generate that sense of rapport because he is a wonderful guy.

How do you think Chris has grown in the role of Kirk over the two films?
He's a confident guy and deserves to be, but he also thinks very carefully about what he is doing. He doesn't take it lightly. His confidence is a much quieter product of his ability, which is prodigious. He

thinks a great deal about every moment. He's very funny also, but he's not sitting around throwing it up there and hoping it sticks because he's a movie star.

The bar scenes between your characters in both films are really pivotal. Did you feel that during the shoot?
Yeah, knowing how critical those scenes are help make them really important. You want to feel every moment is critical for the guy you are playing. Knowing their whole journey was teed-up on the explosion of this relationship, with Pike's death, was highly motivating.

Was it a given you were coming back for *Star Trek Into Darkness*, or did they make you sweat?
Well, I was pretty vocal about wanting to come back. I was also very vocal about wanting to stand up, should I come back (*Laughs*). I didn't want to be that guy who is stuck behind a desk saying, "I told you to go out and do X and you did Y! I'm going to lose my badge if I don't get some answers!" I didn't want to be that Chief of Police; not that that dynamic would ever happen, because these guys are much more careful writers. But I said I was desperate to come back and they said, "I think you will."

I'd check in with J.J. every now and then and he would say, "I would say don't worry about it." With something as oblique as that you think, "Can you give me something real?" I think it was two years before we shot the second one that I knew I was coming back.

So how quickly did they tell you Pike was going to bite it?
It was a hard one. The scripts came out at the last

minute, because J.J. wants to keep it as close to the vest for as long as possible. I got the script and a text from him that seemed a little urgent that said, "Please call me right away before you read the script." I'm thinking, "what happened? Did they send me a script because they promised I'm in it and I'm not in it?"

I called him and he goes, "Have you read it?" I go, "No, I haven't. Should I read it?" He said, "Yeah, you should read it. I want you to know it's not going to be what you suspect." I said, "Oh no!"

He said, "We felt the relationship was so strong that we decided to hang Kirk's quest on the end of that relationship… so you don't make it." I said, "Oh God, no!" But then it took me about 30 seconds, and I'm not kidding about this, to go back to being grateful about being a part of this whole experience with J.J. and the gang.

I'm tremendously fortunate to be part of this. There was literally 25 seconds of "Couldn't you find someone else if there's a third one?", but now that it's all happened and done, I'm in my house thinking, "Didn't someone save a drop of Khan's blood for Pike?" So as a consequence, I think Pike will be very heavy in the third one (*Laughs*).

So you're up for *Star Trek III: the Search for Pike*?
(*Laughs*) Yes!

You did get to do a fantastic *Trek* death scene, which is always more epic than other movie deaths. How many days did it take to shoot?
It took, like, four days to do that sequence, from sitting around the table with all the talk. Then it took three days to do all the action. We spent maybe half a day doing the emotional stuff in the death scene.

What about the scene grabbed you?
That it was emotional with Spock, also. You could sense when he was tapping into what Pike was feeling. It was so good, that with the emotions he really was unwilling to absorb on some level.

You also got to play against Peter Weller's Admiral Marcus – the moral yin to your yang. How was it working with him?
It was fun to watch. A lot of his spiel becomes voiceover when you are looking at the other reactions, but when you watch him doing it, his voice is so mesmerizing. He's got this tremendous tone, those crazy blue eyes, and he's a riveting guy. He's also tremendously interesting to talk to, as he's unconscionably well read. He's one of those guys who brings weight.

Do you feel content that Pike got to finish what he needed to do for Kirk before his goodbye?
No, I think there's room for more conversation, but that's just my deep, deep wish to come back. On any level, I'm not willing to suggest the relationship is finished. It isn't. There's so much that drives the story as there's so much left to be said between the two. You understand how much they care about each other, and you want to see that develop. You want to see Pike actually say, "Go well. You are ready," but we never get there.

You've been in many films and TV shows, so you must get recognized all the time. Has being a part of *Star Trek* changed anything for you in those terms?
I get a lot more double takes. It used to be people come up and would say "*Double Jeopardy*." It's been replaced by "There's Pike!"

With Pike pushing up daisies, where can fans find more Bruce Greenwood?
I'm going on the road to do a musical written by Stephen King and John Mellencamp, called Ghost Brothers of Darkland County. We go on the road in a tour bus. I get to pretend I'm a rock star! ▲

"YOU WANT TO SEE PIKE ACTUALLY SAY, 'GO WELL. YOU ARE READY', BUT WE NEVER GET THERE."

Admiral Pike at home in the big chair (*Star Trek*)

UHURA

● ZOE SALDANA

Main photos © Zade Rosenthal

From a *Pirate of the Caribbean* to a feisty blue alien on a faraway planet, Zoe Saldana is no stranger to playing unusual and strong female characters, but the iconic role of Nyota Uhura is something else, as she explains to Tara Bennett.

Star Trek Magazine: In the four years since you first played Lt. Uhura in Star Trek, how do you feel you've grown or changed as an actress?
Zoe Saldana: The older I get, and the more comfortable I get in my own skin, as me and also as an artist, you shed the insecurity. As the years roll by, you become more confident. You establish a deep intimacy with your characters, and how you feel about the story you are being a part of, so you want to respect a point of view and consider it just as much as the director and fellow co-workers. The older I get, I have been really embracing that.

Since the character first made her mark in the original *Star Trek* television series, she's become an icon for feminism, racial equality, women in science, and more. Did stepping into Uhura's legacy ever feel too confining?
Before I started, I did have those thoughts cross my mind going, 'Oh my God, maybe is this too much pressure?' But [*Star Trek*] was a very light and fun experience. I never felt trapped, or boxed, or prohibited to going to places with my character. We had a lot of freedom, and it was also very good to respect the guidelines of the actors that created these characters before us.

"I DIDN'T WANT HER TO BE BIONIC, AND I DIDN'T WANT HER TO BE WEAK. I JUST WANTED HER TO BE AN EVERYDAY WOMAN WHO IS STRONG."

Uhura at her station on the Bridge

CAREER NOTES

FILMS
Pirates of the Caribbean –
The Curse of the Black Pearl (2003)
Vantage Point (2008)
Avatar (2009)
The Losers (2010)
Colombiana (2011)
Blood Ties (2013)

Zoe Saldana in *Colombiana*

It was a beautiful combination that I guess all of us actors had. It was a beautiful experience. What we had to contribute to our roles was so welcomed by the director, the writers, and all the producers, so it didn't feel like I was limited.

During the press period for *Star Trek*, you had some nice public moments with the original Lt. Uhura, actress Nichelle Nichols. Did you get to just talk as two women who played this important character?
I did. When we were shooting the first *Star Trek* she came to visit, and we were able to talk extensively on set. I felt so humbled by that.

Have you seen her since?
I think the last time I saw Nichelle was, like, two and a half years ago. To see her again would be wonderful. If she is able to go to the premiere, or we can cross paths during press, it would be such a treat for me.

Uhura prepares to take
the *Enterprise* for a dive

You really crafted a Lt. Uhura for a new generation, so what qualities did you want her to possess?
She takes what she does very seriously, and I wanted to showcase that for Uhura. I didn't want her to be bionic, and I didn't want her to be weak. I just wanted her to be an everyday woman who is strong, virile, vulnerable, scared, but also very studious, committed, and responsible. Those were all the traits that I see in women that are in a position like Uhura, and I wanted to incorporate them into her.

In between *Star Trek* films, you did action-oriented films like *The Losers* and *Colombiana*, which allowed you to get very physical. Did those roles help influence how you wanted to play Uhura again?
Well, I don't purposely look for strong, kick-ass roles. I just look for characters of women I would like to be, or I have heard about, or have touched me. I see so much vulnerability and fragility

in every woman that I have ever met, be they family, friend, or stranger. It's just a part of their composition, along with strength and feistiness and sassiness. You don't have to lack vulnerability to be seen as strong. I do believe an honest person, very in tune with their vulnerability, is stronger than somebody who goes through great lengths in order to conceal it. That said, I can see how the characters I have played look strong, and they are strong, but they also have a very weak spot, and that has also been apparent... I hope. [*Laughs*]

So, what's Uhura's weak spot?
I think it's definitely doing her job well, because so many lives depend on it. I thought it was just that at first, but then obviously the relationship with Spock is a very important one for her. I feel like Uhura, along with the other characters in the movie, are compromised because they care so much about what they do.

You were very busy in the interim between *Trek*s, so were you ready to go back into that world?
Yeah, I guess it was good to have a little bit of distance, but at the same time I had such a wonderful experience doing both films that I was ready to come back. It's one of those things, when you have a good experience you want to repeat it.

When you got ready to don the uniform again, was it less nerve-wracking or more because of the success of the first one?
In the second installment, I definitely had more fun. Or maybe I just remember it that way

Uhura worries about Spock's fate in *Star Trek Into Darkness*

because it's the freshest memory that I have. I definitely had a lot of fun with the first one. But with this one, I guess because we were going back to a familiar environment, where we knew each other, and had been through it already, we didn't waste time breaking ice. It was already melted.

Once you finally read the script for *Star Trek Into Darkness*, what was the collaborative process in terms of making suggestions about Uhura's arc, or your character in general?
I think a lot of us had a couple of observations and notes, and J.J. was really open and encouraging for us to speak up, because we incarnated these characters in the first installment. Coming back to it, there were remnants of our characters in us, so if something felt unnatural or a little off, we definitely voiced it, and J.J. definitely considered it.

Uhura: armed and ready

> "SHE'S MORE COMFORTABLE IN HER OWN SKIN, AND FEELS MORE COMFORTABLE WITH HER CREW TO SPEAK UP WHEN SOMETHING JUST DOESN'T FEEL RIGHT."

How was it being back amongst the cast?
We genuinely like each other, and that's wonderful! I have wonderful experiences working on projects where I am able to maintain very healthy relationships with the people who touched me, and are still in my life, and I'm still in theirs. For this experience with *Star Trek*, we were very fortunate as well. There's a child-like energy, overall. We're so excited to be there, and we shared that mood with each other.

Where is Lt. Uhura as a crewmember of the *U.S.S. Enterprise* at this film's start?
She's gotten better at what she does, and is more confident. She's more comfortable in her own skin, and feels more comfortable with her crew to speak up when something just doesn't feel right, from her Captain to her Lieutenant. It was one thing I felt in her, she was definitely more, 'Hey guys, are we really going to do this? Like really?'
I don't think she had that in the first one, because they were just getting to know each other. She is also involved more in the physical

decision-making. She's out of the *Enterprise* a lot more than the first movie, and that's something I hope the fans will like too.

The relationship between Uhura and Spock was a wonderful surprise in the first film. It was so compelling to watch seeming opposites genuinely connect. Are they still together in this film?
Yes, and I think they are trying to deal with those issues as they move forward. They feel comfortable, and because they feel comfortable, they are very honest with each other.

Do we get to see much of their relationship on-screen?
When we're on the *Enterprise*, obviously we are interacting a great deal, and that's pretty cool.

Outside of Uhura's personal arc, what else grabbed you about the sequel's story?
It definitely felt more intense. There was a great deal of suspense and uncertainty, not as actors but for our characters. There's such an attack and infiltration into Starfleet, it makes us question how safe we really are. And then there is the question of who [John Harrison] is and what is this person's intention, because there are a lot of drastic things happening that are so covertly done. It's a very scary feeling. [In *Star Trek*], Nero was a mourning father and husband, so he was walking around seeking revenge because he had a hemorrhaging heart. But this time around, what is [motivating Harrison]? Is it really based out of emotion or ambition? So that is what is questioned by Starfleet and the crew of the *U.S.S. Enterprise* – who are we really dealing with? ▲

MAKING NOTES

Rousing theme tunes are as much a part of *Star Trek* as unexplored worlds and pointy ears, from Alexander Courage's original theme to the majestic score from the 2009 movie. Composer Michael Giacchino reveals the process behind creating the score for *Into Darkness*. Interview by Bryan Cairns

Composer Michael Giacchino is in the eye of the storm. It is mid-February, 2013. His latest endeavor, *Star Trek Into Darkness*, warps into theaters on May 17th, and its music is still in various stages of completion.

With recording to commence on March 4th, most professionals would be experiencing severe panic attacks. For Giacchino, one of Hollywood's most highly regarded composers, these last-minute deadline crunches are par

Images reproduced by kind permission of Michael Giacchino

"THE MUSIC SHOULD
GO HAND-IN-HAND WITH
THE STORY THE DIRECTOR
IS ATTEMPTING
TO ACHIEVE."

Recording the *Into Darkness* soundtrack

for the course. His long list of credits stretch from TV's *Alias*, *Lost* and *Fringe*, to such blockbusters as *The Incredibles*, *Mission: Impossible III*, *Super 8*, *John Carter* and *Star Trek* (2009). Then there's the coup-de-grace, an Oscar for Pixar's *Up*. *Star Trek Magazine* caught up with Giacchino on his way to the studio, and he expressed his hope that the music for *Into Darkness* would once again strike a chord with audiences.

"The key to a successful score is that it's constantly telling the story that is unfolding in front of you, that you're not off on your own, just writing music to hear music, or doing action just to blanket a giant scene," says Giacchino. "The music should go hand-in-hand with the story the director is attempting to achieve."

Giacchino at the mixing desk

TAKE COURAGE

One frequent topic of discussion that echoes that sentiment is Alexander Courage's original *Star Trek* theme. In the prior installment, it played over the closing credits, but so far, Giacchino has no specific plans for it.

"It's a tough thing, because the film has to be in a certain mood to

accommodate a theme like that," he explains. "It's the type of theme you can't just throw in anywhere. If we're going to use it, we really want it to work. What we did in the last film was we used it in a big way, by going over the credits. As of right now, we haven't quite decided what we're doing with the big theme. For me, it is one of my favorite pieces. I'm sure it will present itself in some fashion."

Curious moviegoers already got an earful of Giacchino's score during the *Into Darkness* trailer, and also the nine-minute teaser that ran in front of *The Hobbit*'s IMAX run. Typically, composers view a film once or twice, make notes, and go at it. In the nine-minute footage, Giacchino only had fragments of the final cut with which to work his magic. As it turns out, the process wasn't as disjointed as one might expect.

"The nine minutes we did was a story in its own right," says Giacchino. "It really did tell a specific story. Granted, it left you hanging at the end, but that was the whole point. You want them to come back for more. For me, I had actually seen a lot of the film by that point, and it was just a jumping-off place. Honestly, I'm going back to all of that, and we are going to re-cover that stuff again. A movie is like a living thing. It changes constantly, so what you saw there may not be exactly the way it's used in the body of the film.

"And honestly, I've moved on from that area of the film at this point," he continues. "I just started doing the rest of the movie. Now, I'm at the point where I'm going to circle back and look at this stuff, and see what still holds up or what

"YOU HAVE TO TAKE A SECOND LOOK AT SOMETHING, BECAUSE YOU ALWAYS FEEL YOU COULD DO BETTER."

Director J.J. Abrams with Michael Giacchino

The *Enterprise* awaits her cue

could become better. You have to take a second look at something, because you always feel you could do better. This way, you get a chance to attack it again."

With *Star Trek* (2009), Giacchino had already poured countless hours into delivering a rousing score, full of adventure, heart, and emotion. Rather than discard all those majestic harmonies and start over at square one, he's intentionally building on certain pre-existing arcs and elements.

"The main theme we used in the theme song, we're going to revisit," reports Giacchino. "The theme for Spock will show up now and again. Those are the two main ones that we developed. We'll be expanding on those. There are new characters, of course, like the bad guys. There's a whole new area to explore on this one, which is really fun to see. The last film was basically just trying to get it done, and make everything work as best you can. But now you have a much better fundamental understanding of what the movie is, and what the characters are, and the world that we're creating. Moving forward has been a little easier on this one."

SUITE MUSIC

A frequent collaborator with J.J. Abrams, the two friends have established a groove and, more importantly, a mutual trust when it comes

to their instincts. That means Giacchino had plenty of freedom to explore the sounds and beats he chose to.

"In this one, I did 12 suites of music," he reveals. "Some of them were 12-minute suites, and some were four-or-five-minute suites. I'm basically saying, 'Okay, here's the music I'm envisaging for this character.' Now that I've seen the movie a couple of times, I understand

who these people are, and how their minds work. 'This represents this particular person, and this other thing represents this guy.' Then, when it comes down to scoring the film, it's about saying, 'Yes, we were happy with all this stuff. Now how are we going to keep it within the logic of the movie?' You can't just make that leap and throw it against the movie. It doesn't work that way."

The *Star Trek Into Darkness* orchestra

Michael Giacchino with
Sound Director Ben Burtt

"Although he doesn't show it, Kirk tends to be a little rough," offers Giacchino. "The way he makes up for that are with his bravado, his wit, and strength. For me, it's interesting to explore the underside of that. Not the bold, brassy, heroic side of Kirk. I'm more interested in the side of Kirk that worries about the past, or trying to become a better person.

"Spock, in particular, goes to a place he hasn't really gone before," continues Giacchino. "I don't really want to spoil it, but in the old film it was a chance to explore Spock's heritage and lineage, and what makes him a man. Now, there's another aspect that comes in to play that allows me to use that main theme, but in a very different way. That's been really interesting to me, because it's not just rehashing what was. It's taking what was set up and pushing it further.

"Harrison has a very particular personality in this film, which I can't say much about at this point," he adds. "It's his personality, and the way he thinks, and the way he sees the world. It was very clear to me the type of music that was going to work for a character like that. I had a lot of fun doing him, and thought I had a good handle on what he was feeling inside. That's always the key when you are writing a theme for a character. It's not just what do they look like or what do they do? It's more the things you don't see on screen. What are they thinking when they talk to you?"

Giacchino anticipates that, in the end, he'll generate 90 minutes of music for *Star Trek Into Darkness*. Arguably, the two musical pieces that bookend the movie are the most crucial. One provides a first impression, while the other wraps the story up and leaves people satisfied, or hungry for more. The opening sequence was previewed in the nine-minute teaser, but even Giacchino, as noted, isn't sure what will remain intact.

"I may look at it and think differently on it," states Giacchino. "Right now, the bookends aren't 100 percent clear yet. These are the two areas of film I haven't finished working on, the end and the beginning. All of that is still in flux. I have a general idea, but until I sit down and finish it, God only knows.

"It's interesting," he concludes. "You write the music, and in the end you're watching it with sound effects and everything. There have been times when I've said, 'Let's take out this cue. You don't need that.' I never mind taking music out, even if I spent a lot of time writing it. It doesn't matter to me, because if it makes the film stronger, then by all means, take it out." ▲

Previously, screenwriter Damon Lindelof steered Giacchino in the right direction, stating *Star Trek* was more of a tale between two men than some space scuffle. Those words helped focus his perspective again.

"It's all about the evolution of that friendship between Kirk and Spock," says Giacchino. "It was so nice to have that as a starting point. It's an extension of that. How has it evolved? Also, how does it devolve? What happens along the way, as these two people continue to get to know each other? That's what really interested me, the exploration of Kirk and Spock's relationship. Of course, you have the over-arching story of the film. It was a much bigger path to follow."

"IT WAS VERY CLEAR TO ME THE TYPE OF MUSIC THAT WAS GOING TO WORK FOR A CHARACTER LIKE THAT."

Abrams and Lindelof carefully crafted *Into Darkness* as an ensemble piece that would allow the various characters, from Bones to Scotty, to shine. However, that doesn't necessarily equate into a grand oeuvre for each of them.

"Storytelling really directs what is required," explains Giacchino. "And yes, while all the characters are important, generally, the film will focus on one or two characters. Those are the ones you want to follow, whereas the other characters are supporting that story. They are not off creating their own story, but if they were, yes, they would receive their own theme. *Lost* was a show with a lot of characters, and each of them had their own theme. That was because you were following each and every one of them in a very detailed way."

BOOKENDS

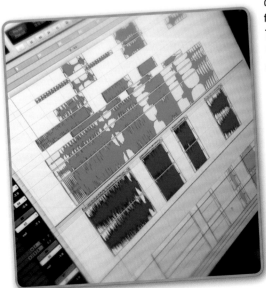

Giacchino did pull out the big thematic guns for Captain Kirk, Spock and resident villain John Harrison, a terrorist with a personal vendetta.

Bones and Kirk run from the Nibiran natives in the opening scene of *Star Trek Into Darkness*

BONE DRY

As a life-long fan of *Star Trek*, playing Leonard 'Bones' McCoy in J.J. Abrams' *Star Trek* (2009) and the hit follow-up *Star Trek Into Darkness*, was a dream come true for Karl Urban. The New Zealand-born actor talks about his love for the show, and his hopes for the five-year mission.
Interview by Christopher Cooper

Star Trek Magazine: When you last spoke to *STM*, back in 2009, you were looking forward to returning to play the character again. Was it easier second time around?

Karl Urban: It did feel more comfortable this time. The first time around, honestly, I was never quite sure where the line was in terms of my contribution to McCoy and honoring my wonderful predecessor, and delivering what I felt to be somewhat of the essence of that.

> ## "WHAT I LOVE ABOUT J.J.'S FILMS IS THE FACT THAT HE'S GIVEN *STAR TREK* A HUGE SHOT IN THE ARM."

Karl Urban with Zachary Quinto, J.J. Abrams and Chris Pine at the *Star Trek Into Darkness* Sydney premiere

Karl Urban as "Bones" McCoy

Simon Pegg, Zoe Saldana, J.J. Abrams, Chris Pine, Karl Urban, Anton Yelchin and John Cho on the *U.S.S. Enterprise* Bridge set

Because it was important to me that the character be recognizably Bones. This time around, I think that I certainly felt a lot more comfortable – I think we all did – and I think we hit the ground running.

Taking on the role of Bones, as a fan was there anything you particularly wanted to echo from DeForest Kelley's performance?
Obviously, I have such a huge degree of respect for the great DeForest Kelley and his contribution to all things *Star Trek*, it's just immense. It's interesting. I think if you put my McCoy side by side with his, you'll see obvious differences, but I think where the two are most aligned are in those iconic moments, the iconic dialogue – "I'm a doctor, not a torpedo technician", for example. When you're in that zone, it feels to me intrinsically Bones.

There's a point where Kirk berates Bones for all his metaphors...
Yeah, that was interesting how that came about, actually. I was looking at my scenes, and I was concerned that every time I spoke, I spoke in metaphors, and I felt that it was a bit overdone. I know McCoy to be a straight-shooter, you know. He tells Kirk what he thinks, and he doesn't give a damn about chain-of-command or ramifications, unless they obviously affect the health and well-being of everybody on the ship.

> ## "J.J. ABRAMS IS ONE OF THE MOST BRILLIANT DIRECTORS THAT I'VE EVER HAD THE PLEASURE TO WORK WITH."

I felt that I was speaking in metaphors a lot, so I went up to J.J. [Abrams] and said, "I've been looking at this scene, and three times in a row I'm speaking in metaphors. Can we drop one of these?" His response to that was to give Chris [Pine] a line pointing out the fact, telling me to stop speaking metaphors. It made a joke of it, which played out particularly well.

When you read the script, there's an awful lot for fans to geek out about, not least the big Khan reveal. How did you feel about that when you read it for the first time?

> ## "FIVE YEARS IN SPACE... GOD HELP ME!"
> McCoy looks forward to the *Enterprise*'s next mission...

I guess my first reaction was 'Wow!' I was a little bit shocked and surprised, and at the same time I was genuinely wondering how the hell we were going to pull this off [*laughs*]. That being said, J.J. Abrams is one of the most brilliant directors that I've ever had the pleasure to work with, and I had supreme confidence that *Star Trek* was in good hands.

You don't get to run around and fight quite as much as the other guys.
Not really, apart from that opening sequence. But I've always liked that – I've played a lot of characters that are very physical, you know, action and fighting, but for me I really relished the opportunity to play a character who was a scientist, who has this wonderful dry sense of humor, this heart of gold, and this irascible shell.

I always found Bones to be the character I most identified with. He's the sort of everyman on the crew.
Yeah, he is really, because when you think about it, there was no ego with him. He was an altruist, and I always identified with him because he was the one that, I guess, conveyed fear, and as a kid I loved watching *Star Trek* because there were episodes that genuinely scared me [*laughs*]. So yes, he's highly identifiable with.

Éomer in the *Lord of the Rings* trilogy gave you exposure around the world. How much of a debt do you owe Peter Jackson?

Obviously, that was a very important breakthrough role, and I'm incredibly proud of being involved in *Lord of the Rings*. Every film you do is as important as each other in your growth as an actor, and I also owe a lot to a little New Zealand film called *The Price of Milk*, because it was that film that Peter Jackson saw, and it was on the basis of that performance that he offered me the role of Éomer.

You shot a TV pilot for J.J. Abrams called *Almost Human*, which has since been commissioned for a full series. What can you tell us about it?

Well, *Almost Human* is set 46 years in the future. It is about a human detective who is coming back to the force after being in a coma for two years, and he is partnered up with a replicant, a synthetic – an android, to use an anachronistic term. The show is about that relationship, and about the exploration of that point in the evolution of humanity where we collectively realize that the genie is out of the bottle, and there's no going back in terms of technology, genetic engineering, the destiny of humanity. Thematically, it's hugely interesting for me, and obviously the opportunity to collaborate with J.J. again was a strong pull.

And you'll have that opportunity again on the third *Star Trek* movie...

Whether he directs or not, he will be involved. He's contracted to produce one more, and I've no doubt that *Star Trek* is in good hands. Even though he didn't direct the last *Mission: Impossible* (2011's *Ghost Protocol*), it was the most

KARL URBAN — STANDOUT FILMS

THE PRICE OF MILK (2000)
Urban plays Rob, a milk farmer who proposes to the love of his life, but she begins to worry the spark has gone out of their relationship. A spate of quilt thefts prompt fiancée Lucinda to resort to extreme measures to get hers back, with disastrous results for their impending marriage.

Karl Urban as *Dredd*

LORD OF THE RINGS: THE TWO TOWERS (2002) AND THE RETURN OF THE KING (2003)
As Éomer, heroic Rider of Rohan in Peter Jackson's epic adaptation of Tolkien's masterpiece, Urban dedicated himself to learning how to control a horse with one hand on the reins, in order to more convincingly wield a sword while riding.

DREDD (2012)
Destined to become a cult classic, Urban plays the ultimate future of law enforcement: Judge Joe Dredd. The movie, based on a British comic strip character created in 1978, pays closer regard to its source material than Sylvester Stallone's 1995 version – and unlike Stallone, Urban's Dredd keeps his Judge's helmet on throughout, in keeping with the original strip.

Bones oversees the unloading of 72 mysterious torpedoes...

Bones takes a blood sample from John Harrison

A METAPHOR TOO FAR

Bones was never a man to hold back his opinions, but he's always been prone to dress them up in colorful metaphors. In *Star Trek Into Darkness*, it seems an under-pressure Kirk has had enough when his friend and confidant criticizes his decision to give Sulu the conn...

BONES

Jim, wait. You just sat that man down at a high-stakes poker game with no cards and told him to bluff. Now Sulu's a good man, but he is no captain.

KIRK

For the next two hours he is – and enough with the metaphors, alright? That's an order.

---

successful one of the franchise, and probably my favorite one of the franchise, so that gives me a lot of confidence on a going-forward basis.

Thematically, the new movie has a lot of resonance with real world events, which echoes the storytelling in the original series. How do you think J.J.'s reinterpretation compares with the original series?
For me, *Star Trek* was always about the characters. It was always a cult of personality. I tuned in because I really enjoyed seeing how that combination of characters would have to work together every week in order to survive,

"AS A FAN, I'M REALLY INTERESTED TO SEE WHERE WE GO FROM HERE."

and the essence of that is alive and well in J.J.'s films. You know, without that attention to detail in the character department, this film wouldn't have the heart and soul that it does. The reason that people really enjoy these films is because they enjoy spending time with the

characters, and they want to see more of them. Like the original, J.J.'s *Star Trek* has a lot of heart, there's good comedy in it, and obviously the action is – no disrespect – completely superior to its predecessors, as are the effects. To me, on a going-forward basis as a fan of *Star Trek*, I feel as long as we get the characters right, and particularly the triumvirate of Bones, Kirk, and Spock, which was at the heart of the series and in quite a few of the movies, then we're on solid ground.

So now you're on the five-year mission, where would you like to see *Star Trek* go next?
What I love about J.J.'s films is the fact that he's given *Star Trek* a huge shot in the arm, fresh adrenalin. He's energized it in a way that *Star Trek* hadn't been energized for a long time – and I'm not disrespecting Robert Wise's *Star Trek* (*The Motion Picture*, 1979), because that's actually one of my favorite *Star Trek*s – but J.J.'s couldn't be more different in terms of pace and energy.

As a fan, I'm really interested to see where we go from here because after *Wrath of Khan*, apart from *The Voyage Home*, [the *Star Trek* movies] had a lot to do with the nemesis, usually a singular being or entity that was the obstacle. It would be wonderful if we can find a way to honor the spirit of Starfleet in terms of space exploration, as well as deal with a clear and present danger. I look forward to simple things, like beaming down to a planet in a landing party with a bunch of red shirts. We'll see! ▲

The Sydney premiere of *Star Trek Into Darkness*

CAROL MARCUS

● ALICE EVE

Main photos © Zade Rosenthal

Oxford graduate Alice Eve plays a young
Starfleet medic destined to become the future
love of Captain James T. Kirk – at least as far
as the original universe is concerned...
Tara Bennett asks how the British actress
made the role her own.

Star Trek Magazine: Obviously, script secrets
about *Star Trek Into Darkness* have been under
lock and key, so as an actor auditioning, how
did the process unfold?
Alice Eve: I got sent some scenes, which I had been
asked to prepare by J.J. [Abrams]. I did that, and

met with him, where we workshopped the material.
The process of working with him was incredibly
rewarding for me, and enjoyable. Then
I spoke to him and his producing partner, Bryan
Burk, afterwards. Maybe 10 days later, J.J. called
and asked me to do the movie.

"THIS CAROL MARCUS THAT I WAS PLAYING, I DIDN'T FEEL SHE WAS TOUGH. I WANTED TO BRING A VULNERABILITY TO HER."

CAREER NOTES

TELEVISION
Hawking (2004)
The Rotters' Club (2005)
Entourage (2011)

FILMS
Starter for 10 (2006)
The Raven (2012)
Decoding Annie Parker (2012)

Alice Eve
in *The Raven*

Carol Marcus and son, David,
in *Star Trek II: The Wrath of Khan*

Had you auditioned for J.J. before, for other projects?
No, I think it was the first time we officially crossed paths.

Did you know you were reading for the character of Carol Marcus? What did they tell you about her?
It was clear at that point it was for *Star Trek*. But no, he didn't tell me it was Carol and, to be honest, that didn't mean anything to me anyway, because I wasn't overly familiar with the universe. He gave me a sense of who the woman was, what drove her, and what her motivations were. All of that gave me enough to create a sketch.

After you were cast, how did you even start the process of diving into 40 years of *Trek* history to understand the universe better?
I did a little skimming, and I found I was drawn

> "J.J. WAS INVOLVED IN ALL ASPECTS. HE WAS EVEN INVOLVED WITH THE COLOR I CHOSE TO WEAR ON MY NAILS."

to the first series, which I found to be so brilliant. I loved watching it. I then watched the first two films, *Star Trek: The Motion Picture* and *The Wrath of Khan*, because Carol appears in it. Then I did some reading, and found some articles on [Roddenberry] and found that interesting. And then, as with all that stuff, you throw away all of it and just get in the moment on the set.

In your research about Carol, what did you discover about the character and how you wanted to play her?
In the original, when she was in *The Wrath of Khan*, she was older and she had a child [Kirk's son, David]. I guess she was tough. This Carol Marcus that I was playing, I didn't feel she was tough. I wanted to bring a vulnerability to her, because she was at the beginning of her journey as a woman, rather than the middle, where she had a child and she's raising him. I wanted to bring that sense of hope and softness to her, along with the list of capabilities that are on the page. And she became mine at some point, I understood that there was a tradition, but I didn't hold too tightly to any of it because she was mine now.

How did you get to read the script?
I went and read the script at Bad Robot, and it was really a privilege to be able to read it from beginning to end. Sometimes at home you get interrupted, or you make some tea, or get a phone call, and there was none of that. It became very clear what the story was in my head, because I read it in one sitting.

What connected you to Carol?
I think she was a human who is highly intelligent and educated. I spent a lot of my early 20s in further education, so I was familiar with that kind of mind. I think she has a specific motivation that was one that I understood and could sympathize with, so both resonated with me quite strongly.

Carol Marcus (Eve) in
McCoy's medical bay

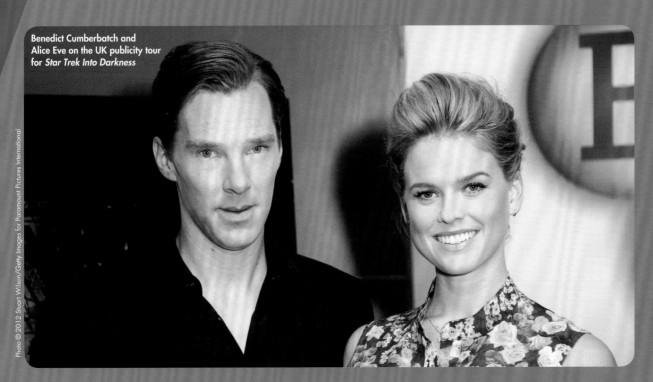

Benedict Cumberbatch and Alice Eve on the UK publicity tour for *Star Trek Into Darkness*

Let's talk about the look of Carol, because fans have sort of obsessed over her retro look in the trailers. How did that come about?
Well, the costumes were already established, so it was understood I was a science officer in the Med Bay, so I would wear blue in sort of the shape of the dress that Zoe [Saldana] wore before. In terms of the hair, obviously this is the future, and there was this interesting debate that raged about what hair was like in the future.

Really?
Yeah, do we have hair? Is it the same hair? Do we color our hair? Is it a helmet? Does it wash itself, and where does it live in the midst of the future? Right now, hair is a demanding thing. You have to cut it and clean it. So whether they had eliminated that was an interesting theoretical. What we decided was that either way, the universal aesthetic that J.J. tends toward is a minimalist one for *Star Trek*. So we used the famous Vidal Sassoon bob from the '60s to build a hairstyle. We think it showed a sense of youth, and it was in keeping with the original imagery of the '60s show, but we modernized it and it added a clean efficiency to the line. It was that stuff we ended up falling on, and J.J. was involved in all aspects. He was even involved with the color I chose to wear on my nails.

You've been featured in two big summer genre blockbusters, with *Men in Black III* and now the *Star Trek* sequel. Did you find working on the two film experiences similar?

I have to say there were fundamental similarities, because the scale is the same on both of them. The only way I can imagine a parallel is when the Romans were moving through Europe and building villages and townships. When you're shooting, there are such a high number of people working at such an accelerated and expert level, that it's like watching something being built from scratch. Another thing that was similar is you walk onto these overwhelming sets, but then it's just you, the other guys in the scene, and the director, just like a play in North London, or an independent movie in upstate New York. When you get down to that, it's the same, and you're just making something together in the way you know how. The brilliant thing about these movies is you have this team of experts, because they add this other dimension, and the finished result becomes overwhelmingly different.

You're one of the new kids in the film, but you worked with Simon Pegg before on the movie *Big Nothing*. Did that help you get comfortable quickly with the cast?
Well, the people behind this film were all so incredible that there was no awkwardness. Everyone knew the reason they were there, and they had clear directives for fulfilling them, and it became a very collaborative process, like building a village. But it was very comforting to have familiar faces when you first go out there, especially the first day. Benedict [Cumberbatch] wasn't there yet when we first started rehearsals. I guess he was cast later. I knew Benedict, but to have Simon in the room when I got there was nice and comforting.

Simon is very caring, and made me feel very comfortable, not that everyone else wasn't equally welcoming, but it does make a difference.

In past *Trek* mythology, Carol and Kirk become lovers. Without spoiling your arc in this film, you are obviously a part of Kirk's *Enterprise*, and right in the thick of the emotional journey.
Yes, I am, but it's not always about Kirk. There are very heavy emotional journeys that we went on, but I think the most challenging thing for me was running around the *Enterprise* (*Laughs*). I had funny shoes, and I felt like I was running always, and everything was very high intensity.

What was one of your favorite memories of the shoot?
I have to say it wasn't me, but I went to this [location] and saw Benedict doing some wire work. I've known Benedict for nearly nine or 10 years now, and I saw him flying through the air! It was just amazing to see that. It was staggering to see your friend working in that way, with all these people around. It was dusk as well, in this weird location and I was thinking "this is crazy."

Now, with the filming done and some distance from the part, how do you feel about the character of Carol, and the experience overall?
I know that I admire her tenacity, and her bravery. It's always great to play someone you can learn from. I think the characters you are drawn to hold things that are unexplored in yourself. I definitely knew that Carol was braver than I was when we started, and more tenacious. I hope I've learned from her. ▲

SCOTTY

● SIMON PEGG

Main photos © Zade Rosenthal

One of British film and television's biggest comedy exports, Simon Pegg is also a life-long *Trek* fan. His turn as Chief Engineer Montgomery Scott was a highlight of J.J. Abrams' revitalized *Star Trek*, and he's excited to be rejoining the crew as they head *Into Darkness*...
Interview by Christopher Cooper

Star Trek Magazine: You're back as Scotty for a second time. Without the worry of fans accepting a new cast, was this second voyage a more comfortable experience?
Simon Pegg: Yes, absolutely. Your first concerns are obviously with how you're going to do it, not how everyone else is going to feel about you doing it. Having kind of eased into the roles, and all got to know each other as actors, and become friends, it was actually something we all really relished and were excited about doing. It was like a school reunion. We all

bonded on the first film, and then it was suddenly over, so to get to do it again, and do it with J.J., was a great joy.

Your performance as Scotty is very energized. Was there anything you took from Doohan's performance?
Well, James Doohan played the role for many, many years, and you saw my Scotty in one situation, and it was a highly energizing situation (*laughs*). I'm sure there were episodes of the original series where Scotty was a lot more histrionic than I was in that film. It just

"I WAS SO GRIPPED BY
THE SCRIPT. I REMEMBER
LITERALLY LEAPING UP AND
DOWN IN MY HOTEL ROOM
AT CERTAIN PLOT TWISTS
AND REVELATIONS."

Scotty reports
on the situation

CAREER NOTES

TELEVISION
Six Pairs of Pants (1995)
Big Train (1998)
Spaced (1999)
Doctor Who (2005)

FILMS
24 Hour Party People (2002)
Shaun of the Dead (2004)
Hot Fuzz (2007)
Paul (2011)
World's End (2013)

Simon Pegg in *Paul*

happens that my first appearance as Scotty was in the midst of an insane situation with Nero, and also having been stranded on my own on a planet for six months, or however long I'd been there. I always tried to approach the role in the same way that James [Doohan] did, which was to look at who [Scotty] was, what he did, and evaluate the circumstances he was in at the time. None of us are doing impressions of the actors, cause we're not playing actors, we're playing characters. All of us approached it in different ways. Karl [Urban] definitely took on the gruffness of Bones, because that was Bones' signature thing, and he wanted him to be recognizable. Unfortunately for me, Scotty is admittedly someone people can hang a peg on, if you'll pardon the pun.

Is Scotty again the main comic thread for the film, or do you get a bit more drama this time?
There's much more drama this time, I think, but don't forget in the first film Kirk was running around with giant, fat hands, so Scotty's not just there to be the funny guy. Scotty, by his very nature, is slightly more of an everyman, he often will react to a situation as we would. He's less cool than Kirk, he tends to react emotionally to stuff, so if something weird is going on he won't just raise an eyebrow and shoot someone, he'll go, "Wow! What the ****'s happening here?!"

Like the scene in the middle of the movie, where Scotty is behind enemy lines and needs to open an airlock door. You do a lot of running. It's thrillingly exciting, as well as being hilarious.

That's one of those. It's another one of those moments where, if there wasn't some lightheartedness, it would probably be quite uncomfortable to watch, as there's a lot riding on that moment.

I remember that day very clearly, 'cause I'd just eaten and I rocked up on set and J.J. said "You've got to run 100 meters, really fast." And I did, three times in a row, and then I threw up.

I'd been hanging around all day on set, it was a nice shoot, I'd had a big dinner, then they say "OK Simon, you're up", and I had to do this sprint. And I did it as fast as I could. I mean, I really went for it. I did the first take and everyone clapped, because I ran like I hadn't run since I was a kid. It was amazing. And then J.J. said "Can we do it again?" and I said "Yeah! No problem!" By the third take I was, like, "No." So I went back to my trailer and got rid of the mezzé. Fortunately, my trailer was a simple stumble away.

Was it a fun set?
It is larky, yes, but it's never intensive because we work hard and fast, and J.J. works hard and fast, so you've got to concentrate. But it's always a very lighthearted environment, and J.J. is a brilliant leader. He keeps everything so buoyant, so even at the hardest points everyone remains upbeat. It's a good environment to work in. We have lots of fun. Me and Chris Pine have a great laugh. We spent a lot of time together on this, and we had a hoot. It's most fun when we're all together, cause it's a very familiar environment, and welcoming Alice Eve and Ben Cumberbatch was great, because we wanted them to feel as welcome as we did.

Scotty performs a
tricky feat of transporting

Uhura, Scotty and McCoy on the Bridge in *Star Trek Into Darkness*

With Karl Urban being *Dredd*, Benedict Cumberbatch as *Sherlock*, and Zachary Quinto as Sylar in *Heroes*, it's an increasingly geek-pleasing cast. As a self-proclaimed geek, have you had a bit of a geek-fest working on these films?

Not really. I mean, when we're all together, we're sat playing "Words With Friends", not talking about our various affiliations to fantasy worlds. It's always amusing to us, to know that between us we inhabit many, many fan-person environments, but it never really comes up. We don't talk about work, we do other things.

How would the young Simon Pegg feel about your career now, and of being in *Star Trek*?
It's not something he could ever have imagined happening.

I always try and imagine what my seven-year-old self would have thought about it. I'm sure he'd be incredibly excited and impressed – I am, when I look at it. I've loved *Star Trek* since I was about nine years old, and to become part of it was an extraordinary privilege. I remember one of the most incredible things was working with Leonard Nimoy on the first film. Getting to act with him as Spock was incredible. I was interacting with a character I had known since I was nine years old, for 30 years, and there he was, with the ears, talking to me and saying "You are Montgomery Scott." I don't know if there's another situation where you could possibly go through that. It was quite amazing. I don't ever want to lose that sense of wonder about it all, otherwise it would become boring.

> ## "IN THE FIRST FILM, KIRK WAS RUNNING AROUND WITH GIANT, FAT HANDS, SO SCOTTY'S NOT JUST THERE TO BE THE FUNNY GUY."

How are you feeling about *Into Darkness*?
It's a great story. I read the script in New York, at the end of [2011]. I was with a friend of mine, and I said, "Listen, I'm going to quickly go up to my room. I've got the script, I might read the first couple of pages, then I'll come down and we'll go Christmas shopping." About five minutes later, I

Scotty has some worrying news

rang him and said I'm not coming down (*laughs*), 'cause I was so gripped by the script. I remember literally leaping up and down in my hotel room at certain plot twists and revelations that were just so exciting, and so cool. So then to get to shoot that, and see what J.J. came up with, the amazing work that's done by costume and props and make-up – it was all really exciting.

As a writer yourself, how was the experience of working with Bob Orci, Alex Kurtzman, and Damon Lindelof?
I wrote to them after I read the script, because there are bits in there that I really got, I could see what they were doing, and there were really smart little touches that I wanted to know that I'd got. It's always really nice to read the work of writers who you appreciate. You can see the mechanics of it, and also be surprised by them.

It's a hell of a task they've got on their hands. They've got to juggle a lot of things – they've got to please fans and entertain the uninitiated – but I think this film has all that. There are so many rewards in it if you're a fan of *Star Trek*. You could watch this movie completely uninitiated and be thrilled by it. You don't need prior knowledge, but if you do have that prior knowledge then it's like it unlocks a whole other dimension of connection with *Star Trek* that you'll feel very privileged to have.

You've done zombies and extra-terrestrials, but you've not yet written an all-out space movie of your own. Are you tempted?
Yeah, if the story's right, and the script's right. I'd never say no to a space movie. I love 'em! ▲

SULU

● JOHN CHO

Main photos © Zade Rosenthal

Since 2009, actor John Cho has steered a successful course through television projects, films, and fatherhood, but it's good to be back at the controls of the *Enterprise*, as he explains to Tara Bennett.

Star Trek Magazine: You've been a part of the *Star Trek* family for four years now. What has surprised you most about the fandom?
John Cho: I guess with *Star Trek*, what was surprising to me was the revelation of just how broad the fanbase was. I probably would have guessed it, but it's another thing to meet so many fans of so many ages, backgrounds, and nationalities. It means so much, to so many different kinds of people. It's a wonderful shock to realize it.

Back in 2008, when you first stepped into the Sulu role, what was most prevalent in your mind with regards to how the fanbase would respond?

I was afraid that if they didn't like me, or they didn't like our film, they would be mean. And maybe the people who didn't like it, or me, would come up and tell me. (*Laughs*) When they like you, I feel like *Star Trek* fans are the warmest, so if you do right by them, my experience is they will shower you with affection. But you have to do right by them.

What allowed you to relax and embrace the opportunity and make this Sulu your own?
I was lucky, going into it with a director I trusted. I had a sense [J.J.] had it under control. When you start going to rehearsals and seeing

"I THINK THE FACT THAT WE GET ON IS SOMETHING THAT TRANSLATES ONTO THE SCREEN, AND PEOPLE CAN SMELL THAT IT'S REAL."

Sulu: more than just a fencer

things, and you read the script, you see it's achieving two significant objectives. One was tipping our hats to the original series, and then also trying to strike out in our own direction. I think all of the indications were that he was achieving those two goals beautifully. I felt comfortable then, relaxing in what I was doing and letting him worry about it, and I was just having fun with everyone else.

What did you want to imbue in your version of Hikaru Sulu that felt integral to the character?

At the time, I was thinking about vitality, and making him active. If there was one thing that I wanted to see different about the original series it's that I wanted George [Takei] to be up and out of his chair more often, and part of the action, so maybe, subliminally almost, I was just trying to push energy into the character. I was also trying to remain in the realm of a person who could become George Takei. I thought that an impression of him would not be good for me. His literal voice is so unique, and like none other, that if I started doing that

Sulu takes the helm of the *Enterprise*

voice I would look like an ass. I was like, 'Okay, remember don't do that.' (*Laughs*) Although at one point with J.J., I went too high with my register, and he came up to me and said, "I think you should pitch that down a little bit."

You were very busy between the *Trek* movies, working in films and TV shows such as your current series, *Go On*. Did you appreciate the downtime, or were you itching to get back to the *Enterprise* Bridge?

I wanted to go right back into it! I think we were waiting for a homerun script, and J.J. was undecided. Scheduling was tight, and it didn't really get settled until J.J. decided he could do it. I would have gone right [back]. It's a longer layover than most [sequels], considering the first one did so well, and that there was sequel talk instantly. We were wondering about the second picture almost as soon as we were finished with the first, so it seemed like a long time. But in the meantime, everyone did different things. Life happened. Children were born. It felt like a long time, but when we got back to set it felt like it was an afternoon at best, because we all got right back into things.

Did you spend any of that time pondering Sulu's future in the next film?

No. That sort of thing, I realized, is not in my control, nor is it my forte. I felt that they did right by Sulu in the first movie, so I was preparing myself to be pleasantly surprised when I read it, and I was.

Once you got to read it, what impressed you most about the sequel story?

Sulu on the *Enterprise* Bridge in *Star Trek Into Darkness*

I felt like the themes they were trying to tackle really spoke to me. The movie is so much about morality; what the nature of good and evil is. How does that change when one grows older and is more experienced? It's tapping into the grey areas of life. As a comparison, the first movie is a young man, and the world is a simpler place, where actions and reactions are black and white. The second movie is an older person, a legitimate man, and life seems cloudier and sloppy, so decisions are harder to make. I thought that was wholly the appropriate tone for a second film. It was really fascinating to me, because in some ways you expect an interesting plot, thrilling action, and fun, but going deeper in that fashion is not necessarily expected. I thought, thematically, it was ambitious.

What is Mr. Sulu's challenge as a member of the *Enterprise* crew in the sequel?
I think Sulu's challenge here is to rise to the occasion. It's intentionally vague, but he has to meet his own level of ambition.

Any physical challenges for Sulu?
I would say so. (*Laughs*) There's a tight suit involved; it's an uncomfortable suit. Even the Bridge uniforms are pretty slim fit. It's never slouch wear. [Costume designer Michael Kaplan]'s also very meticulous about wrinkles. There are no wrinkles in the *Star Trek* universe he's created.

Why am I imagining Kaplan stalking Sulu on the Bridge with an iron?
Yes! It's not an exaggeration. (*Laughs*)

"THE MOVIE IS SO MUCH ABOUT MORALITY; WHAT THE NATURE OF GOOD AND EVIL IS."

One of the universal comments from your cast is how much you all bonded in the first film. Your group rapport translated to your characters too. Do you think that is a big reason why audiences accepted you all so well in the classic roles?
I don't know why, but I feel like people can sense whether a relationship is true or not. It's not like we had to spend weeks in boot camp together, like they did for *Platoon*, to prove we are a unit. I think the fact that we get on is something that translates onto the screen, and people can smell that it's real. It is real, and doesn't necessarily make the film good or bad, but it helps the audience buy that these people care for one another, and that they work with one another, and that they know one another. With a disparate group of people that doesn't always happen. It's more likely to happen when you have a strong personality doing the casting – that would be J.J. Abrams – and he's our intermediary. Everyone struck a chord with him, and I think that's something that connects all of us through J.J. and maybe that's why we get along well. Or maybe it's because we are the only ones on set dressed the way we are. (*Laughs*)

There was some new cast as well. Did you get to work with or befriend any of them?

I got to know Alice Eve (Carol Marcus) very well, and she's one sharp tack. She came in and fit right in. Another quality everyone seems to have [in the cast] is that everyone is pretty smart. Fart jokes aside, we get into some stuff off-camera. She jumped right in there. She's so smart, interesting, and obviously easy on the eyes. She was a pleasure to know, and it kept the set lively to have to get to know another person.

What are you most excited for audiences to experience in this sequel?
I spoke about some of the thematic elements, but I'm also excited that if they haven't gotten to know a fellow named Benedict Cumberbatch, they are about to. He is a formidable actor and a lovely friend. People are going to be excited about his performance. He's amazing.

Do you think he lands a place in the *Star Trek* villain Hall of Fame?
I would say that, but the only reason I would back off that comment is that there have been so many great villains. I would say confidently he can more than hold his own with the villains of the *Star Trek* universe. He's really passionate and intelligent, and it comes off in his performance. You can see the gears turning, and he's a fascinating person to watch.

Are you hoping there's less time between this film and *Star Trek* 13?
Yes! We should have done it *Back to the Future* style, back-to-back, and as a Western too! ⋀

CHEKOV

● ANTON YELCHIN

Main photos © Zade Rosenthal

Anton Yelchin is well immersed in the three Rs of Hollywood: Reboots, Remakes, and Relaunches. The rising star has taken on metal monsters in *Terminator Salvation*, matched wits with a vampire neighbor in horror-comedy *Fright Night*, and is now back on the *Enterprise* as enthusiastic officer Pavel Chekov in the *Star Trek* sequels.
Interview by Bryan Cairns

Star Trek Magazine: Looking back at *Star Trek* (2009), what was your interpretation of Chekov? What traits were crucial in capturing his essence?
Anton Yelchin: The Chekov created by Walter Koenig is so full of joy. Everything from his physicality, to the intonation of his delivery. It's such a joyous character and so much fun to watch. That's really what I studied for the first one, and what I wanted to bring to my version of the character. To me, I was quite happy how he turned out. It felt like he was a very joyous

character, yet there were times he was really grounded in the gravity of what was happening, and you got that as well. You got that in the *Trek* films, more than the shows, so I felt it was all there. He wasn't just a one-dimensional character.

Anticipation was high for this *Star Trek* relaunch. How gratifying was it when it was embraced by critics and fans?
I had a lot of gratitude for the fact it was well-received, but I think when you are shooting –

"EVERYTHING IS BIGGER. THE COMPLEXITY OF THE EMOTIONS IS BIGGER. THE DECISIONS THE CHARACTERS HAVE TO MAKE ARE BIGGER."

Chekov changes shirts
in *Star Trek Into Darkness*

CAREER NOTES

TELEVISION
Taken (2002)
Curb Your Enthusiasm (2004)
Huff (2004)

FILMS
Hearts in Atlantis (2001)
Alpha Dog (2006)
Terminator Salvation (2009)

Anton Yelchin in *Terminator Salvation*

even when you know there is all this pressure, and you acknowledge that – you cannot dwell on that or it will prevent you from doing the best job that you can do. If you dwell on tension while you're working, your mind isn't completely on the work. You trust your captain, J.J. Abrams, who is magnificent. Having worked with him, and spoken with him, and seen his work, that trust was very much justified, and proved to be the case when the film came out.

The main cast is all back, but J.J. Abrams returning was never a guarantee. Were you a bit relieved when they announced he would be directing?
Oh, definitely. Just for the joy of working with him. I trust J.J. immensely and everyone around him, like Bryan Burk. They are very smart, and talented, and respectable people. Whatever decision they make, I've always had the utmost respect for them.

Chekov reflects upon life
aboard the *U.S.S. Enterprise*

But for the pleasure of working with J.J., and the talent and insight and vision he brings to things, of course I was so excited. It was wonderful to know he was coming back to shoot it. It wouldn't have been the same without all the same people there. Literally, the operators were the same. The sound crew. I saw people four years later that I hadn't seen in ages. It was like this big reunion.

Can you take us back to the first time you read the *Into Darkness* script? What was your initial impression?
I think I was actually able to read it at home, which I wasn't allowed for the first one. But I loved it. It's like the first film, but with a bigger scope. Everything is bigger. The complexity of the emotions is bigger. The decisions the characters have to make are bigger. The conflict is bigger. The tension is bigger. Because you are not burdened with, "Okay, now I have to introduce all these guys,"

you are able to up the ante in terms of what's happening, and the world they are in. I don't just mean physically, but emotionally. You are able to explore everything more intensely. The script had the same kind of humor and warmth, and emotional accuracy to the situations and complexities these characters are going through, while building on the action elements of the film. It was just a more powerful version of that first film.

Where do the darker elements of the sequel come into play?
What the tone stems from is the decisions the characters have to make. Because Kirk's decision now isn't, "Am I going to join? Am I not going to join?" He's already the Captain. Now it's about how a Captain relates to the crew, and the decisions the Captain is willing to make. Also, the way the crew responds to those decisions. That is already a much more complex relationship. Once again, what J.J. does brilliantly is introduce both drama and comedy in this in a way that doesn't feel forced. He lets you breathe when you need to breathe, and yet, he delivers these things that have this emotional weight and feel very real.

Were you looking forward to reprising your role as Chekov? Did it give you a deeper understanding of him?
Very much so. I love this character. I was really looking forward to getting back into studying what makes Chekov him, and then explore that in the context of this crew, and explore all our characters together again. For me, it was trying to recapture the same physicality and joy I see in Chekov, in accordance with what was happening.

Chekov takes orders from
Kirk in *Star Trek Into Darkness*

In the trailer, Chekov is sporting a red uniform instead of his trademark gold shirt. Does that mean he's been promoted? How have Chekov's responsibilities changed?

All I can say is, in accordance with the intensity of the character relationships, everybody's responsibilities in this film, for each other's lives, have increased.

How was it stepping back on to the *Enterprise* set and wearing the Starfleet uniform again?

It was wild. It was so wonderful and strange. When we got together, it sounds clichéd, but it felt like yesterday. You know when you don't see friends for a while? The best version of getting together is when there is no awkwardness and you feel like you're back where you left off. That's exactly what it was. The difference was last time we were playing a lot of chess, and now we're playing "Words With Friends" [the word-based board game].

Sitting in those seats, and remembering, "Oh yeah, this is what it's like...." It was a lot of fun.

One of Chekov's signature traits is the Russian accent. Was that easy to slip back into?

I loved the accent, and what Walter did with Chekov. I just tried to remain as truthful to that as possible. Coming back to the accent, I just re-watched Walter's work and, weirdly, I re-watched our film, which I probably hadn't seen since it came out. I revisited this world, and you start to plug things back in. You go, "Wait a minute. How do you say 'Captain?' How do you say 'Sir?' Because certain things are

"I LOVED THE ACCENT, AND WHAT WALTER DID WITH CHEKOV. I JUST TRIED TO REMAIN AS TRUTHFUL TO THAT AS POSSIBLE."

obvious. Sometimes they write the dialogue in Chekov-sound. They did that in the first one too, with the "w's" and the "v's." When I looked back, it was funny, because huge chunks of dialogue were still in my mind. I would just recall those on set and apply them.

In the previous installment, Chekov saved Kirk and Sulu from the freefall. He figured out how to beam on board Nero's ship undetected. What's interesting about making Chekov this young, quick-thinking genius?

It allowed me to play the fun of having a lot of responsibility at a young age, and offering up some of the moments of comedy Chekov has always had in *Trek*. That's just another way of looking at who Chekov is, and how he's taking on his responsibilities. In this one, he's still the youngest, obviously, but it allows you to find new moments. That's really what it is on a film like this.

How challenging was the *Into Darkness* shoot compared to the last one?

There were more things in this one that were physically demanding. There were more worlds they visited. The sets they built were greater in number. The *Enterprise* itself had more to the ship. As a practical set, to walk down one hallway and it doesn't turn into green screen, it just keeps going. It had a much bigger scope in general, and was therefore more physically taxing for everyone. That also applies to how taxing it was emotionally. Everything is pushed to the limit.

***Star Trek* (2009) was a worldwide blockbuster. What impact did that have on your career and life?**

For me, it's one thing to be part of a film that's very successful, but it's a greater thing to be part of a good film, and something you can be proud of, and not say when you're going back to the sequel, "Oh, it's also going to suck." You're saying, "I'm going back to the second one, and I think we're going to make an even better movie. And the first one was already great." It's exciting to be part of something that is so well done, and has such great people, and people that I respect and enjoy being around. When people see it and you receive recognition for it, it allows you to go on to other things and at the same time, retain your contentment or respect for what you've done.

What are your expectations?

I have such huge confidence in what J.J. accomplished. Just from the trailer, I was blown away. It already looks more epic than the first one. I know what happens in it, and I've seen the performances, and they are wonderful. This movie is going to be amazing. ⏶

> "I COULDN'T IMAGINE WRITING A LOVE SCENE IN WHICH THE CHARACTERS CALLED EACH OTHER BY THEIR SURNAMES."
> VONDA N. MCINTYRE

A NOVEL APPROACH

THE ART OF TRANSPORTING A MOVIE ONTO THE PRINTED PAGE

As *Star Trek Into Darkness* arrives in movie theaters with great fanfare, another take on the film's top secret storyline will make its debut on bookshelves, Kindles, and e-readers, in the form of its tie-in novelization. John De Gruyther talks to fan-favorite authors Vonda N. McIntyre and Alan Dean Foster, and finds there is an art to recreating a movie with words alone.

Movie novelizations don't tend to receive much critical attention, but nowadays they play a key part in the promotional campaign for any major movie. Each time a *Star Trek* movie has been released there has been a literary adaptation, and as is often the case with *Star Trek*, the franchise seems to bring something different to the party, defying that very idea of the tie-in novel being simply another marketing tool. What makes the *Star Trek* tie-in novels stand out compared with other tie-ins is the deep connection the authors have with the *Trek* universe, and how they understand its significance to people.

To convincingly portray the events of a movie in novel form is a specialist skill, and one of almost infinite possibilities, given the size and scope of the *Star Trek* universe. Those authors chosen to adapt each movie into book form are entrusted with shaping and informing the back-stories of *Star Trek*'s much cherished characters, often even influencing developments on the show itself. Therefore it should come as no surprise that for the 12 movies (including *Star Trek Into Darkness*)

there have only been four novelists. In chronological order, the authors have been: *Star Trek* creator Gene Roddenberry (who is credited as writing the novel for *The Motion Picture*), Vonda N. McIntyre (*The Wrath of Khan*, *The Search for Spock*, and *The Voyage Home*), J.M. Dillard (*The Final Frontier*, *The Undiscovered Country*, *Generations*, *First Contact*, *Insurrection*, and *Nemesis*), and most recently Alan Dean Foster, who penned both 2009's *Star Trek* adaptation, and the novel version of *Star Trek Into Darkness*.

But what exactly lies behind the process of bringing a movie to life within the pages of a book? *Star Trek Magazine* sought out a few words of wisdom from those who know best: the *Star Trek* novelists themselves.

EXPANDING THE UNIVERSE

One of the most popular films of the franchise, *The Wrath of Khan* seems a good place to start, being both critically acclaimed and a fan favorite. The book version, published in 1982 and written by Vonda N. McIntyre, is a great read and a real collectors' item for any fan of the show, as it contains several fascinating differences to the film. McIntrye also holds a unique place in *Star Trek* history as the lady who gave Mr. Sulu his first name. 'Hikaru' Sulu came into being as a consequence of McIntyre writing a love scene for the dynamic helmsman, in her *Trek* novel "The Entropy Effect", as she explains, "I couldn't imagine writing a love scene in which the characters called each other by their surnames. It would be silly. So for Mr. Sulu's given name I snatched the name of the hero of one of the first novels ever written, *The Tale of Genji*, by the Lady Murasaki. From 12th Century Japan, if I remember right."

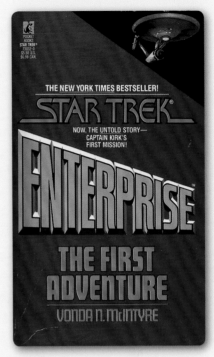

This logical and seemingly innocuous literary decision then became part of *Star Trek* canon;

"Years later I found that the scene had caused quite a stir between Paramount and Pocket Books, because Mr. Sulu didn't have a first name in the original series. The person vetting the manuscript at Paramount balked. My editor had the good idea of asking Gene Roddenberry and George Takei what they thought, and they both liked it, so the book, and the love scene, and Mr. Sulu's given name went ahead. I knew nothing about this till years after the book was published. Years after that, another sci-fi and tie-in writer (Peter David, if I remember right) was on the set of one of the movies and mentioned Mr. Sulu's given name in the book, and apparently the director added it to the movie on the spot. This story is second or third-hand though," she admits.

VONDA N. MCINTYRE: TOP FIVE

Five classic SF movie novelizations adapted by Vonda N. McIntyre

Dreamsnake (1978)
Fireflood And Other Stories (1979)
Star Trek: The Entropy Effect (1981)
Enterprise: The First Adventure (1986)
The Moon And The Sun (1997)

Scotty's nephew, Peter Preston, gets more screen time on the printed page

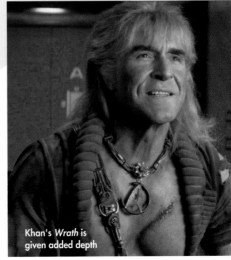

Khan's *Wrath* is given added depth

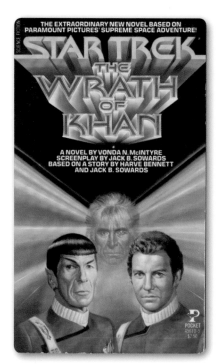

McIntyre is a veteran of science fiction writing, and this has helped her create stories full of great character detail, whether read in conjuction with the movie or in isolation. McIntyre's *Trek* novels are enthralling, and she shows there can certainly be creativity in the process of the movie novelization, should the author want it:

"If you transcribe a movie screenplay, you get at best a novella, which is about half the length of a modern novel. To create a novel from a screenplay, you have the choice of padding mercilessly or adding subplots and back-story," the author explains, "I was fortunate in being trusted to add subplots and backstory, and to treat the characters and the universe with respect. Merciless padding tends to be boring, both for the writer and the reader. The difference

in inherent length between a movie and a novel is why many movies made from novels are unsatisfying to fans of the original novel. I learned this firsthand when I wrote a screenplay 'The Moon and the Sun' at a writer's Workshop at Universal and Amblin. The whole time I was writing the screenplay, I had to leave out all sorts of wonderful information, so I promised myself a novel when the workshop ended. The novel I ended up writing is about 120,000 words long and went on to win the Nebula Award".

Clearly, a key part of the process for the tie-in author is expanding on the page what the movie didn't have time to say. For example, *The Voyage Home* novel has time to detail the aftermath of the death of David Marcus, and how Carol Marcus and Captain Kirk grieve the loss of their son. In the movie version of *The Wrath of Khan* we meet minor character Peter Preston, intended to be Scotty's nephew in the original screenplay. His appearances on screen are brief, and the character dies in the final scenes. In McIntyre's book, you get a much fuller backstory for Preston, making his death far more emotive. Preston appears in two scenes in the movie, in

comparison to the book, where he features on 28 pages, including an amusing scene with Admiral Kirk featuring a "left-handed spanner". In the same book we also learn that Spock's Vulcan protégé, Saavik, was in fact half-Romulan. It is these additional scenes and details that make the tie-ins so much fun, and well worth reading.

As McIntyre explains, some of the major differences that occur can be down to what version of the screenplay the author works from. "Peter Preston had more screen time in the screenplay I was working from. If I remember right, I believe I added the graveyard scene. So I expanded that character's arc somewhat, but not as much as it would seem if you compared the movie and the novel rather than the screenplay and the novel. I made up most of Saavik's backstory. Does the movie even mention that she's Romulan and Vulcan? I blush to admit I can't remember. That was in the screenplay. Her flirtation with David Marcus ended up mostly on the cutting-room floor, but it was also in the screenplay I worked from. I expanded it a little."

LICENSED TO CREATE

The particular challenges faced by the tie-in writer from classic era *Trek* to the modern era have clearly eased because of the advent of electronic media, and the fact that the tie-in has become an accepted part of the commercial machinations of promoting a movie. Novels like *The Wrath of Khan* and *Search for Spock* are curios from a bygone era, based on previous versions of screenplays that were never filmed, and featuring story arcs imagined by creative authors. The studio gave them little thought and as a consequence the writers had a greater licence to expand.

Novelizations now hold a much more prominent place in the thoughts of the studio, influencing

> ## "I ALWAYS WORKED FROM THE SCRIPT. THIS WAS NOT NECESSARILY THE SCRIPT THAT ACCURATELY REPRESENTED WHAT ENDED UP ON SCREEN."
>
> VONDA N. MCINTYRE

The Voyage Home novel explores the aftermath of the death of David Marcus

the way they interact with and support the novelist. Certainly, the assistance a writer can expect to receive has improved since the days of *The Wrath of Khan*. As McIntyre explains with wonderful clarity, back then it was clear where the tie-in ranked in the studio's priorities.

"I always worked from the script. This was not necessarily the script that accurately represented what ended up on screen. Once in a while, mainly for *Wrath of Khan*, I had a few production stills. Usually if I asked for information, I would get sent a publicity picture of William Shatner as Captain Kirk. This was less than useful because, as you might imagine, I know what William Shatner as Captain Kirk looks like," says McIntyre with a smile. "Remember that we're talking about a time before most publishers had digitized their book-producing process, and everything was still done on paper galleys and page proofs. Getting galleys and page proofs back and forth took more time than it does now with email. Because of differences in the way books were produced and movies are produced, the manuscript had to be finished well before the movie was done. I never saw any

of the movies before the manuscript had to be turned in, or indeed until the movies came out in the theater. I've never been to a *Star Trek* movie set. The producer, screenwriter, and director have many more things on their minds than talking to the tie-in writer."

READING IN THE DARK

There is still scope for imagination and creative license in the modern tie-in, as evidenced by the current post-holder of 'official *Star Trek* novelist,' Alan Dean Foster. Foster is a prolific tie-in author, responsible for countless novelizations for a myriad of movie franchises. Foster's work epitomizes that special "something" that *Trek* novelizations seem to have. He has the deep knowledge of the characters needed to be successful in this field, and is steeped in the history of *Star Trek*. He wrote the story for the movie *The Motion Picture*, and in a twist of continuity, is now responsible for the novelizations of 2009's *Star Trek* and its follow-up, *Star Trek Into Darkness*. He explains how his involvement with *The Motion Picture* came about.

"Roddenberry was soliciting story treatments from a number of writers for a proposed revival of the TV series. I was among them because of my work on the *Star Trek Log* books. I submitted several ideas, including one based on a two-page note of Roddenberry's called 'Robot's Return'. It was decided to open the new series with a two-hour movie for TV. Then Paramount decided to do a movie instead of a revived TV show. My extended treatment was chosen as the basis for the film."

The actual process of creating the novel itself varies depending on the author's preference, and with the studio now having more of a say in the tie-ins' content, you can be forgiven for thinking that there is less room for the author to have much poetic licence to expand scenes, or introduce more elaborate back-stories. This,

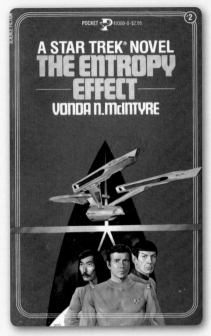

however, can vary, as Foster recounts from some of his experiences, "I usually get just the script. Sometimes I have access to some pre-production drawings or stills. In the case of the two recent *Star Trek* films, however, I have been able to view a version of the actual film, which is of course very helpful. I set the script to one side of my computer, read a bit, change from screenplay format to prose, and expand where it strikes me as suitable and interesting to do so, and as long as it doesn't directly contradict anything happening on screen, I usually have a fair amount of freedom to expand." As to whether some studios are more flexible than others, Foster is forthright; "It varies from complete freedom (*Star Wars*, *Alien*, *Riddick*) to overbearing interference (*Alien 3*)."

His last official involvement with *Star Trek* may have been over 30 years ago with the

ALAN DEAN FOSTER: TOP FIVE

Five classic SF movie novelizations adapted by Foster

Dark Star (1975)
Star Wars: From The Adventures Of Luke Skywalker (1976)
Alien (1979)
Outland (1981)
The Last Starfighter (1984)

An even more eventful
Voyage Home in the novelization

STAR TREK III
THE SEARCH FOR
SPOCK
VONDA N. McINTYRE

and less archetypes. Scotty's drinking, Uhura's emotions, Chekov's youthful uncertainty... For a writer, these allow more development, and also more story options."

The world of *Star Trek* literature is a vast one and the passion for the stories told, whether on screen or on the page, is clear when you read any of the books. This is particularly evident when you talk to anyone directly involved, and this dedication to creating rich and detailed stories is one of the things that make *Star Trek* so unique. So whether it is extra plotting you are after, un-restricted-by-budget space battles, or just more emotional interplay between your favorite characters then, thanks to the skill of the tie-in author, the movie novelizations have everything you could wish for. If you are not sure where to start, then *Wrath of Khan* by Vonda N. McIntyre is highly recommended, and is a great launch into *Trek*'s literary world, as it encapsulates all that is great about these novels. So next time you go to watch a *Star Trek* film, make sure you pick up a copy of the tie-in novel as well – it will be worth it. ⌃

Hikaru Sulu – the name is canon in any universe

novelizations of *The Animated Series*, but he is glad to be back in a universe he enjoys, writing for some of his favorite *Trek* characters. "I enjoy writing all the characters, and I have a soft spot for McCoy, who would rather be fishing, but doesn't let it affect his job." Foster now has a unique insight into the new movies, and he is categorical in what is good about them as movies, and interesting from his perspective as the tie-in author; "I thought all concerned have done a fine job of rebooting the franchise. As soon as I saw the first one, I knew it would be successful because it was a good movie. The fact that it was *Star Trek* was incidental. I think one of the real pleasures of the rebooted series is the opportunity for everyone involved – Abrams, the actors, the writers – to let the characters be more human, more individual,

> ## "I THINK ONE OF THE REAL PLEASURES OF THE REBOOTED SERIES IS THE OPPORTUNITY FOR EVERYONE INVOLVED TO LET THE CHARACTERS BE MORE HUMAN."
> ALAN DEAN FOSTER

Spock rediscovers himself in *The Voyage Home*

Saavik and T'Pau watch the crew depart

STAR TREK
INTO DARKNESS

STAR TREK SCRAPBOOK

THE CELLULOID FRONTIER

After a decade-long mission on syndicated television, 1979 saw the original *Enterprise* crew finally reunited on the big screen. Mark Phillips scans the trivia archives to uncover rare and unexpected stories charting *Star Trek*'s transition to the silver screen, from *The Motion Picture* to *The Undiscovered Country*.

Kirk returns in
The Motion Picture

A t an early *Star Trek* convention in the mid-70s, Gene Roddenberry agreed to take part in a "50-Question Quiz" on the series he'd created, but as he sheepishly confessed to Bob Thomas of *The Associated Press* in 1978, "I only got four out of the 50 questions correct." One bewildered fan couldn't understand how the Great Bird of the Galaxy could have flunked the quiz so badly. Wasn't he supposed to know everything about *Star Trek*?! "I don't talk *Star Trek* at home," Roddenberry explained. "I'm not a guru. It frightens me to see 10,000 people treating a script I've written as if it were scripture."

Roddenberry was understandably nervous, because *Star Trek* was on its way back, though not to

TV. Buoyed on by the box-office success of *Star Wars*, Paramount Pictures had decided to kick the years-in-development TV revival *Star Trek: Phase II* into touch, and announced plans for *Trek* to return as a major motion picture in 1979, with the company's incumbent president Michael Eisner admitting "This should have happened back in 1975."

One critic pointed out to Roddenberry the risks involved in bringing a long-dead television show back to life as a movie, citing the movie remake of the 1958-61 *Peter Gunn* TV series, produced by Blake Edwards and starring original lead Craig Stevens. *Gunn* (1967) had tanked at the box-office and bombed with the critics. Roddenberry quickly changed the subject.

"Khhhaaaaan!"

Boldly venturing onto the big screen

STAR TRIVIA

Gene Roddenberry said that when he saw long lines for *Star Wars* outside a San Diego movie theater in 1977, he was amazed by how many fans' faces he recognized from past *Star Trek* conventions. Although he was disappointed that *Star Wars* had beaten *Star Trek* to the big screen, he admitted, "I've seen *Star Wars* four times already and I love it!"

As J.J. Abrams would later discover when relaunching the movie series in 2009, *Star Trek: The Motion Picture* had a mountain to climb in the face of fan and critical expectation. Even before the movie went into production, the film's director Robert Wise received mail from fans demanding that nothing be changed from the original 1960s TV series. Those same fans would no-doubt have been horrified had they known that a no-show from a certain Vulcan science officer was on the cards. Robert Wise would later reveal that the original screenplay did not include Mr. Spock, as actor Leonard Nimoy had already declined to take part in *Phase II*. Wise's wife and daughter, both *Trek* fans, warned him in no uncertain terms "No Spock. No film," so he pushed hard for Nimoy's participation. Thankfully a deal was reached with the actor, but in other areas Wise was insistent that the movie be allowed to be a movie. "What was okay for the TV show is not okay for the feature," he said, when refusing to use the *Enterprise* sets already constructed for the decommissioned *Star Trek: Phase II* series, because they didn't "measure up" to feature film standards.

Wise also faced a running battle with the powers-that-be at Paramount during post-production. "Every time I heard that they wanted to cut out the scene with Captain Kirk in 23rd Century San Francisco, I screamed!" said the legendary director. "It is very important that we show the Earth in this film."

In another parallel with the 21st Century *Star Trek*, a great deal of secrecy surrounded production of *The Motion Picture*. When *The Associated Press*' Jerry Buck visited the movie's sets, he found security guards everywhere, special passes required, and he learned that one man had been convicted for stealing top-secret

Sulu and Chekov watch the *Enterprise*'s demise in *Star Trek III*

Dame Judith Anderson in *Star Trek III*

Gillian and Kirk in *Star Trek IV*

blueprints of the new *U.S.S. Enterprise*. The ship's gleaming set interiors took up more space than three football fields, and Buck observed, "This *Enterprise* makes the old spaceship look like a prize out of a crackerjack box!"

The film went on to be a worldwide hit, and *Star Trek* as a movie series was born. Robert Wise was pleased but exhausted. "For my next picture, I want a simple script, a small cast and conventional sets!" he begged.

ANGER MANAGEMENT

When Harve Bennett was hired to produce the second film, he had to admit that *Star Trek: The Motion Picture* had bored his kids. "They kept asking to go to the bathroom or to buy popcorn," he recalled to Dale Pollock of the *LA Times*. Hoping to take *Star Trek* back to its roots with the

second movie, Bennett screened all 79 original episodes to find one that might be worthy of a sequel. He considered revisiting "Charlie X" but later revealed "the one episode I could not forget was 'Space Seed'." He became excited over the dramatic possibilities posed by following the villainous Khan Noonien Singh's fate after being deposited on Ceti Alpha Five by Captain Kirk. *Star Trek II* had not only found its villain, but its title – *Star Trek II: The Wrath of Khan*.

Ricardo Montalban, tired of his current TV role as Mr. Roarke of *Fantasy Island*, relished the opportunity to reprise his Khan role, but in early rehearsals he was shocked that his performance as Khan kept coming out as the bland Mr. Roarke. "It dismayed and disturbed me," the frustrated actor confided to *The Montreal Gazette*. "I would have been laughed off the screen." So he watched "Space

"STUDIO EXECS WERE RE-ASSURED THAT EVEN WITH SPOCK'S SHOCKING DEMISE, *THE WRATH OF KHAN* WAS DESTINED FOR SUCCESS."

Kirk's son, David Marcus

STAR TRIVIA

Although not stated in *Star Trek: The Motion Picture*, Will Decker (Stephen Collins) was supposed to be the son of Commodore Matt Decker (William Windom), who sacrificed himself to "The Doomsday Machine" in the original series. Windom, although not a *Star Trek* fan, did watch *Star Trek: The Motion Picture* and was aware that Will was "my son." After seeing Will sacrifice his life to *V'ger*, Windom admitted he left the theater, "pouting over the loss of my boy!"

The time-traveling
Bird of Prey in *Star Trek IV*

As a young model working in London in 1970, former Miss India Persis Khambatta had wanted to fly to America to guest-star on her two favorite TV shows, *Star Trek* and *Mission: Impossible*. She was devastated when her agent called to say that *Star Trek* had been deader than a red shirt "for over a year," but Khambatta's dreams were realized when she was cast as *The Motion Picture*'s sensual alien, Ilia.

However, the trauma of having her head shaved for the role left her in tears. When a humorless restaurant manager demanded that Khambatta remove a scarf covering her head because she was attracting too much attention, Khambatta complied, revealing her magnificently bald head. The other diners gasped in astonishment and then burst into applause. Khambatta told writer Colin Dangaard that if *Star Trek: The Motion Picture* was a success, she would sell each strand of her shaved hair for one million dollars each!

Seed" four times in a row, and by the third viewing he "remembered" how he had played Khan back in 1967 – and all remnants of Mr. Roarke disappeared.

Controversy raged behind the scenes over Spock's fate during the movie's finale, as rumors of the character's death spread across fandom. But when a preview audience in Kansas stood up and cheered as the credits rolled, studio execs were re-assured that even with Spock's shocking demise, *The Wrath of Khan* was destined for success. The movie's debut broke box-office records, and the many good reviews included one from *Time* magazine's Richard Schickel, who gushed, "It's like catching up with old friends."

SEARCHING FOR DIRECTION

Nimoy agreed to direct *Star Trek III: The Search For Spock* (1984) and offered the role of the

Vulcan high priestess to Dame Judith Anderson, an 86-year-old classical theater actress. She made him laugh by confessing she had no idea what *Star Trek* was. But her nephew was a devout fan and he would not forgive her unless she took the part. "To show me what *Star Trek* was about, they screened the second film to me in an empty theater," she recalled to *Associated Press*. "I was terrified – and fascinated – by it."

Bob Thomas of *AP* liked *The Search For Spock*, saying it "stresses friendship, loyalty and good deeds," but David Elliot of *Copley News Network* found it disappointing, and observed that Klingon heavy Christopher Lloyd's forehead "looks like a failed pottery project."

Nimoy returned to direct what would be the most successful classic *Trek* feature, *Star Trek IV: The Voyage Home* (1986). "It's time to lighten up

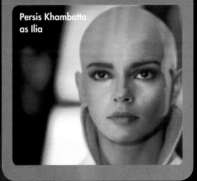

Persis Khambatta
as Ilia

Discovering 1980s San Francisco

Kirk, Bones and Spock camp out in *Star Trek V*

Kirk climbs Yosemite mountain

Kirk and McCoy on trial in *Star Trek VI*

Spock and half-brother, Sybok

"IF A SEVENTH *TREK* FILM WITH THE ORIGINAL CAST WERE MADE, SPOCK WOULD GET MARRIED AND CAPTAIN KIRK KILLED."

and have some fun," said Nimoy. The original idea was to either have the crew travel back to the prehistoric days or to the 1890s for a western adventure. The final version had the crew end up in modern San Francisco to rescue endangered whales. During filming, *Knight Rider*'s Glenn Lovell saw Shatner and Catherine Hicks engage in a vigorous sword fight in a restaurant... with breadsticks! Hicks, who played Dr. Gillian Taylor, was so inspired by the film's "save the whales" theme that she joined a conservation group and adopted a wild whale named Isis.

Critics loved the movie. "It skillfully blends light entertainment with a serious ecological message," raved *The Syracuse Post-Standard*.

Roddenberry called *The Voyage Home* his favorite *Trek* movie to date. "It's great fun and Nimoy has done a fine job of directing it," he said.

ROW, ROW, ROW YOUR BOAT

With *Star Trek V: The Final Frontier* (1989), Shatner was able to fulfill his "secret desire" to direct. The crew meets Spock's half-brother Sybok (Laurence Luckinbill) as they search for God. Luckinbill had never seen *Star Trek* before, even though his mother-in-law, Lucille Ball, had once swept sand from the set of "Where No Man Has Gone Before" in 1965 to speed up its production (she had co-owned Desilu, *Star Trek*'s production studio). After sharing a plane flight with Patrick Stewart in 1988,

Spock hunts for a traitor in *Star Trek VI*

Luckinbill watched with sympathy as Stewart was surrounded by enthusiastic *Star Trek* fans after leaving the plane, while a grateful Luckinbill enjoyed walking out the exits in anonymous silence, but a year later he admitted he enjoyed the attention from fans as Sybok.

Luckinbill tore off his alien ears at the end of every day and threw them away, but he noticed Nimoy always carefully removed his ears and put them in a box. "Otherwise, people will play fast and loose with my ears," Nimoy told reporter Paul McKie. Nimoy donated the ears to charity auctions.

The Final Frontier received very mixed reviews. *The LA Times*' Kevin Thomas praised it "as much of a spiritual odyssey as a space adventure," but Joan Waterfield of *The Lethbridge Herald* found it lacking. "I miss the original show's imagination, with its tribbles and beloved Horta."

The final *Trek* with the original cast, *Star Trek VI: The Undiscovered Country* (1991), was directed by Nicholas Meyer and dealt with Kirk and company engaging in "peace talks" with the crumbling Klingon Empire. Betsy Pickle of *Scripps Howard News Service* said the cast found it "eerie" by how it paralleled the "real meltdown" of the cold war between the U.S. and Russia. Nimoy, who shared story credit, noted, "Our script was originally art imitating life, and it is now life imitating art." He truly believed this was going to be the last film with the original cast. "This is really intended as a goodbye movie."

The Undiscovered Country received glowing reviews from Marshall Fine of *Gannett News Service*. "It's a credible and intriguing finale with speculative fiction firmly rooted in the concerns of today." The

The original crew bid farewell

Gainesville Sun noted, "The crew may be a little long in years but they still have plenty of lift-off." Columnist Chris Hicks reported rumors that if a seventh *Trek* film with the original cast were made, Spock would get married and Captain Kirk killed. Paramount instead signed the *Next Generation* cast to continue the big-screen versions. Meanwhile, Shatner admitted he had taken Kirk's celebrity "somewhat lightly" but with *Generations* (1994) he was "saddened" that his iconic role was over.

As Picard and crew set off their own big screen voyages, we finally said goodbye to the original *Star Trek* cast who, through their six movies, had accomplished their cinematic space mission: to live long and prosper. ⏶

REALITY CHECK

A year before he was even born, actor Chris Pine already had a connection with *Star Trek*, albeit obliquely. On a 1979 TV show called *Match Game*, his father, actor Robert Pine, appeared as a celebrity panellist. Sitting across from him was a young contestant, a pretty interior designer from Wichita, Kansas. When host Gene Rayburn mis-pronounced her first name as Kristie, Kirstie Alley sharply corrected him. Kirstie, future star of sit-com *Cheers* and Spock's protégé Saavik in *Star Trek II: The Wrath of Khan* not only won the top prize (with the help of Pine senior, whom she leaped out of her chair to kiss), she impressed viewers with her natural poise and beauty.

A dedicated Spock fan as a young girl, Alley told *The Winnipeg Free Press* that she won the role of Lt. Saavik "by doing all of the same Spock mannerisms I had done as a kid – the raised eyebrow, the works." When asked, "How do you like your Vulcan ears as Lt. Saavik?" Alley quipped, "Actually, I like them much better than my own ears!"

When an underground Los Angeles newspaper published an advertisement from a prostitute named Rita, a mix-up over phone numbers saw the paper publish Kirstie Alley's unlisted number instead of Rita's. This resulted in the actress getting a series of unsavory phone calls from men desperately seeking Rita. Alley got so sick of the "unpleasant" calls that she recorded a message on her answering machine: "This is not Rita and I do not do what Rita does."

Kirstie Alley as Saavik

STAR TREK: THE MOTION PICTURE
THE ORIGINAL STAR TREK REBOOT

Star Trek: The Motion Picture went through many changes during its development, but one of the few constants was the presence of associate producer Jon Povill, who reveals the trials and tribulations of bringing *Star Trek* to the silver screen...

Interview by Ross Plesset

Jon Povill's involvement with Gene Roddenberry began long before *Star Trek: The Motion Picture*. In 1972, when fresh out of UCLA film school, Povill wrote a feature adaptation of Robert Sheckley's short story "Ticket to Tranai." Although written for a young Ron Shusett (of *Alien* fame), Tranai became Povill's sample script, and being a *Star Trek* fan, he presented it to Gene Roddenberry.

Roddenberry was impressed enough to let the young writer submit a story idea for his proposed series, Questor. Although this project never got beyond the pilot, The Questor Tapes, Povill continued to work with Roddenberry in a variety of capacities, including as researcher, handyman, and gofer. He brainstormed with Roddenberry and did research for a novel which, while never finished, became incorporated into the *Star Trek* universe as the basis for The God Thing (the first of many unsuccessful attempts to revive *Star Trek* in live-action).

In the ensuing years, Povill recalls, "I was there for all the failed attempts to make a *Star Trek* movie. I wasn't in a place where I was in any way considered key personnel, I was just sort of a fly on the wall for all of it. I talked to Gene about it. [Prospective screenwriters] Chris Bryant and Allan Scott were very receptive to me, and I hung out with them quite a bit when they were working on it. They were extremely frustrated because, for the life of them, they couldn't figure out what anybody was trying to achieve with this thing."

During these years, Povill also "spent endless hours talking to Gene about *Star Trek*, about its philosophy and my own take on how we get to the 23rd Century versus where he was at on it." Povill's outlook, which was vastly more optimistic than Roddenberry's, would eventually become incorporated into both the planned *Star Trek* revival TV series *Phase II* and *Star Trek: The Next Generation*. His personal experiences with Roddenberry and knowledge of *Star Trek* also made him a valuable asset for the Phase II series when it went into development in 1977 and eventually, at the behest of writer-producer Harold Livingston, Povill became the show's story editor. When Paramount decided not to proceed with *Phase II*, replacing it with what became *Star Trek: The Motion Picture*, Povill stayed on as associate producer.

ALTERED IMAGE

Star Trek Logs writer Alan Dean Foster had been invited to submit a treatment for the two-hour pilot for *Star Trek Phase II* (reprinted in Garfield and Judy Reeves-Stevens's exhaustive account of the making of the aborted series). Although Foster would receive a screen credit for the story, his script, "In Thy Image" (based on an idea by Roddenberry entitled "Robot's Return") differed considerably from what became the storyline for *Star Trek: The Motion Picture*. Povill recalls that the ending in particular was a problem throughout the process.

"The ending was the biggest issue because there were a lot of different incarnations," he points out, "and none of them were satisfying for a big movie

> ## "THE DISPLAY OF SPECIAL EFFECTS WAS ESSENTIAL TO IT, BECAUSE THE STUDIO FELT THAT THAT WAS WHAT MADE IT A BIG MOVIE."

or even as a pilot. The droopy daisy argument (where Kirk says: "Look, I drew a droopy daisy, I understand why this is art, you don't. Ha-ha!!") and the tricking of the computer had been done in earlier episodes, and the whole 'robot's return' had been done as well. So we really needed something that took it some place different so that it was unique and special.

"What I did was to look at it from the perspective of V'Ger. The idea that it was coming back to seek its creator was there, so what I added was essentially my personal modus operandi: it wanted to see its creator because it wanted to evolve. It wanted to become like its creator, it wanted to get to the next stage of its existence. I think that all sentient beings are essentially looking to advance themselves. And so V'Ger had to have a plan. After talking to NASA, I discovered the ground test computer, and that gave us the device by which this could be achieved.

"V'Ger had a plan to use the ground test computer to get the Creator to come to it. Once the Creator was there, V'Ger would be able to capture the Creator and join with Him. A lot of that kind of got lost in the feature, but it's actually all there."

The debate continued throughout production of the movie, leading to delays as different viewpoints were expressed. At one point V'Ger was going to be exposed to sounds and images representing humankind, including our dark side, at which point V'Ger would have given humanity all the information it had collected. However, Povill couldn't see how that could become

Alien *Enterprise* crewmembers

STAR TREK
THE MOTION PICTURE

After a vast cloud of energy destroys three Klingon warships on its way toward Earth, Admiral James T. Kirk retakes command of the newly refitted *U.S.S. Enterprise*, much to the consternation of Will Decker, who was to have been the new captain. On Vulcan, Spock's search for inner peace is interrupted as he becomes aware of the crisis. However, after rendezvousing with the *Enterprise* he is strangely aloof, unable to reconnect even with Kirk. Spock reveals he has sensed a powerful consciousness emanating from the cloud, which he believes will provide him with the personal answers he has been seeking.

As the *Enterprise* intercepts the cloud, a probe invades the bridge and replaces the ship's navigator, Lieutenant Ilia, with a robotic duplicate so that the intelligence behind the cloud – which identifies itself as V'Ger – may study the crew. A distraught Will Decker, who loved the original Ilia, discovers V'Ger is traveling to Earth in search of "the creator."

Spock succeeds in mindmelding with V'Ger and discerning its true nature as a stagnant machine intelligence. When the *Enterprise* reaches the heart of the cloud it is learned that V'Ger was once *Voyager 6*, a lost NASA probe that was found and augmented by a planet of living machines before being sent back out to complete its mission of exploration. Somehow achieving sentience in the process, V'Ger now seeks its creator in the hope of transcending its original purpose. Failing that, V'Ger will destroy Earth.

Will Decker volunteers to act as a surrogate, a representative of humanity with whom V'Ger, through its Ilia-probe, may merge toward a new state of being. Decker is successful, saving his ship, his crew, and his world. The *Enterprise*, with Kirk in command, a newly-centered Spock at his side, sets off on its next adventure.

V'Ger

JON POVILL

Original *Star Trek* fan Jon Povill started his career in association with series creator Gene Roddenberry, who solicited treatments from Povill during the 1970s when the first attempts were made to develop *Star Trek* into a motion picture. When the studio's focus temporarily shifted to reviving the series on television for *Star Trek Phase II*, Povill became a story editor based on a script he co-wrote entitled "The Child." Povill also collaborated with Roddenberry on the *Phase II* series bible. When *Phase II* was abandoned in favor of reviving a feature film version of *Star Trek*, Povill was hired as an associate producer.

When "The Child" was revised and produced in 1988 for *Star Trek: The Next Generation*, Povill and his original collaborator on the script, Jaron Summers, received writing credit for the episode.

In the 1990s, Povill shared credit on the screen story for the movie *Total Recall*, and later became a producer and script consultant on the science fiction TV series *Sliders*, for which he also wrote three episodes.

In 2008, Povill and Summers's script for "The Child" was produced again for the fan-made series, *Star Trek New Voyages: Phase II*, and directed by Povill.

anything more than a series of random images. "That was exactly the point that I had raised to [director Robert] Wise when that was being proposed, and that was, in fact, what Paramount wanted," he explains. "We were supposed to get all the information that V'Ger had collected through its years traveling through the galaxy. I said to Bob: 'What does that look like? What is it? How are we going to have any response to it?' It just made no sense to me that we were going to see a bunch of images that we could not possibly relate to and have any kind of emotional reaction to it whatsoever. It was totally unsatisfying."

"THE ENDING WAS THE BIGGEST ISSUE BECAUSE THERE WERE A LOT OF DIFFERENT INCARNATIONS, AND NONE OF THEM WERE SATISFYING FOR A BIG MOVIE."

The other problem was that all the recent big science fiction films, with which Paramount knew *Star Trek* would be compared, ended with a large effects sequence. "The display of special effects was essential to it," Povill notes, "because they felt that that was what made it a big movie. And that was part of why they finally went to my ending: the visualization of the meld was a beautiful-looking ending."

The Motion Picture climaxes with Commander Will Decker joining with the Ilia probe created by V'Ger, in part because Decker believes that Ilia is still somewhere within V'Ger after being absorbed earlier in the film. "That was very much Robert Wise's intent," Povill agrees. "He wanted that feeling of a love story, and I didn't learn that until the Director's Cut. I had lobbied very, very hard for him to change the order on the shots to make sure that we understood the plot point of V'Ger capturing the Creator and that the process of the capture had to begin immediately when Decker punches in the code, or the continuity of the entire story gets blown because we don't see that V'Ger is reacting to that. But Bob wanted to emphasize the love story element of it. He felt that was more emotional and more important, and so he went that way.

"I don't necessarily agree with it, but you're never going to get me to say a negative word regarding Bob Wise. The picture didn't get made without Bob Wise. He did monumental work on it. It was such a difficult job, and he deserves so much more credit than he gets for it. It did not do great things for his career, but he was just fantastic; and he was very, very smart; and very, very talented, and if he wanted to end the film that way, it was certainly his right."

LOSING CONTROL

The problems behind the scenes on *Star Trek: The Motion Picture* are well documented, and Povill says bluntly that "Once Bob Wise came on the scene, Gene no longer had command of the show. It wasn't his any more. There was a constant power struggle within the production, and it was very trying on all of us. Everybody has ideas, and there were tremendously talented people on that movie. In most of the cases, everybody had the best of all possible intentions. They had their vision, and they were trying to get their vision realized for the best of all possible reasons, but the opinions were highly divergent. So it was very, very difficult to try and generate a coherent vision of the whole.

"That was Bob's job, and he was constantly trying to get everybody onto the same page without stifling anybody's creativity or input. I think it was hard for Gene to not be The Guy on it, whereas he certainly was The Guy on Phase II. But at the same time, it was being realized as a big motion picture, and that probably felt pretty good. Plus he was making more money on it."

Star Trek: The Motion Picture marked the first time that the franchise had returned to Earth, and a number of Roddenberry's visions for the planet were lost during the production process. In Harold Livingston's first draft script, for example, much of San Francisco has been consumed by nature but by the final film, much of what we see of Earth almost looks like the inside of a mall.

Starfleet Command, San Francisco

"In the shot of the shuttle coming in, there was a lot of green area," Povill says, "but you don't get a strong sense of anything except Starfleet Headquarters there – which doesn't give you the full sense of what Gene was talking about, I agree. It would have been nice if Gene's vision had been better incorporated there. I think that would be a beautiful thing."

Discussing his reaction to the finished film, Povill admits that he "can't look at anything that I've worked on and not have grave reservations. I look at something, and see what's wrong with it more than I see what's right. I continue to want to make things better all the time. God knows I was not pleased with it. I felt it was slow. I felt that the whole Jonah in the Whale idea of the *Enterprise* being trapped inside V'Ger was not pulled off at all in the visual effects. The interior of V'Ger was supposed to be hard-edged and metallic. We were supposed to feel claustrophobic in there, we were supposed to feel utterly and completely trapped. Instead, we were in a cloud – big deal!

"There has to be a hard, finite edge so that you remember that we are inside, that we are trapped. The Bob Abel drawings for what V'Ger was going to look like in the interior that came from, I think, Richard Taylor were what we thought we'd have, visually. They were just concept drawings, but that's what was in our minds, and that was working!"

Unfortunately, the movie was scheduled for release on a set date in December 1979 which could not be changed under any circumstances, and so "what was released was a rough cut, a rough cut with effects that were not nearly what they were supposed to be."

ALMOST A COMPLETELY NEW *ENTERPRISE*

When people talk about the 2009 *Star Trek* feature film and how it reinvented the franchise, comparisons are often drawn with *Star Trek II: The Wrath of Khan*, the film most often credited with "saving" and revitalizing *Star Trek*. But the first attempt to revise the series for the big screen, *Star Trek: The Motion Picture*, was in many respects a more ambitious reinvention than its more popular sequel, and its influence on the franchise to come should not be overlooked.

For starters, *TMP* introduced significant and permanent changes to the characters of Kirk and Spock. Its portrayal of James Kirk as a man who would take on the Starfleet establishment and do whatever it took to get his way (in this case retaking command of the *Enterprise* and pushing aside its new captain Will Decker) laid the groundwork for the "maverick" reputation Kirk developed in the later films.

More fundamentally, while the Spock of the original series was troubled and torn between logic and emotion, his mind meld with V'Ger in *TMP* enabled him to reconcile the halves of his nature and grow into the serene, self-assured individual he has been ever since, from *ST II* all the way to the 2009 film. Additionally, *TMP* was first time a member of the core ensemble (Chekov) was given the role of security chief, a precedent followed by all subsequent series.

While the original series' visual effects and art direction were cutting-edge for 1960s television, it was still a low-budget show. *TMP*'s extraordinary visual effects and elaborate production values raised the bar for all subsequent *Star Trek* productions. Aspects of the *Enterprise* refit – hull plating, glowing nacelle grilles and deflector dish, distinct torpedo tubes, docking ports, and maneuvering thrusters – continued to influence all subsequent Starfleet designs. The sets and corridors became

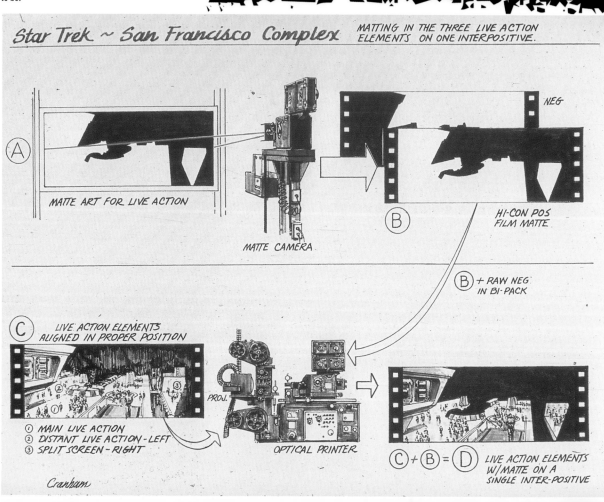

Star Trek ~ San Francisco Complex MATTING IN THE THREE LIVE ACTION ELEMENTS ON ONE INTERPOSITIVE.

Ⓐ MATTE ART FOR LIVE ACTION

MATTE CAMERA

NEG

Ⓑ HI-CON POS FILM MATTE

Ⓑ + RAW NEG IN BI-PACK

Ⓒ LIVE ACTION ELEMENTS ALIGNED IN PROPER POSITION

PROJ.

OPTICAL PRINTER

① MAIN LIVE ACTION
② DISTANT LIVE ACTION - LEFT
③ SPLIT SCREEN - RIGHT

Ⓒ + Ⓑ = Ⓓ LIVE ACTION ELEMENTS W/MATTE ON A SINGLE INTER-POSITIVE

Cranham

a mainstay of *Star Trek* productions for decades. *TMP's* adoption of the *Enterprise* "arrowhead" as the insignia of all Starfleet became standard in every subsequent production, even retroactively in the 2009 film.

However, the more fundamental ways in which *TMP* attempted to reinvent *Star Trek* did not always last, and many were even undone by *ST II*. The original series, partly by design and partly by conceptual drift, had been a mix of sophisticated adult drama and melodramatic space-opera action. In *TMP*, Gene Roddenberry and Robert Wise angled more toward the former, aspiring to elevate *Star Trek* to the level of a cinematic epic, a sophisticated, rarefied, and thought-provoking work of science fiction along the lines of *2001: A Space Odyssey*. After *TMP's* disappointing performance, *The Wrath of Khan* shifted the balance in the other direction. The epic scope was replaced with a tightly budgeted approach managed by veteran television producer Harve Bennett. The erudite, intellectual style was replaced with rollicking action, larger-than-life melodrama, and fanciful sci-fi gimmickry in the vein of *Star Wars*. All subsequent *Star Trek* films were expected by the studio to be heavier on action and spectacle than drama and philosophy, sometimes to their detriment.

Still, *TMP's* influence remained, particularly when Roddenberry brought *Star Trek* back to television with *The Next Generation*. While *TNG* was obligated to maintain a level of action matching the audience expectations created by *ST II*, it was otherwise more like *TMP* in its sedate, intellectual approach to its characters and ideas. Indeed, some of *TNG's* characters were directly recycled from *Phase II*, the failed TV revival project that evolved into *TMP*. Will Riker and Deanna Troi were a revamped Will Decker and Ilia, and Riker's relationship with Picard was modelled on *Phase II's* planned interaction between Decker and the older, wiser Kirk. Data, while largely based on the title android of Roddenberry's 1973 television pilot *The Questor Tapes*, owed just as much to *Phase II's* Xon, a Vulcan science officer who aspired to understand and explore humanity.

What might *Star Trek* have been like had it continued in the vein of *TMP*? Probably less successful in the long run. But perhaps it might have gained a classier reputation as a film franchise, one that aimed for a more thought-provoking level and was more dependent on characters and philosophy than explosions and fights. If Paramount had continued to entrust *Star Trek* to prominent directors like Wise, refining the potential of *TMP's* approach rather than abandoning it after one flawed attempt, the films might have gained at least critical success. In that case, they might even have served as a counterbalance for the influence *Star Wars* had on public perceptions of science fiction, showing that the genre allowed for sophisticated, idea-driven drama as well as visceral action and spectacle. Perhaps the genre as a whole might have gained more respectability. But *Star Trek* itself might not have been as large a part of it.

Christopher L. Bennett

REVISING THE PAST

Robert Wise revisited the movie 20 years later, with the release in 2001 of his Director's Edition, re-cutting sequences, and taking advantage of the massive improvements in special effects. "The Director's Edition helped," Povill says. "It's the best cut of it that I've seen. Even so, it's still long and doesn't necessarily generate the kind of edge-of-seat tension that we all had hoped for. And some of the dialog still annoys me. The reintroduction of the characters, which was so important to us, I think goes on too long. I think they did it better in the new movie. It needed to have been done a lot more economically."

If *Star Trek Phase II* had continued, the Deltan Lt. Ilia would have been a recurring character (as would Will Decker). During the development of the TV series, Povill had devised clear plans for the species. "My concept for the Deltans was that they were essentially the anti-Vulcans," he explains. "They are emotionally advanced; they utilize their emotions the way Vulcans use logic. They choose to experience and process their emotions to the fullest, and it gives them great strength and great life. They are connected in ways that we can only dream of. The reason for the oath of celibacy is not because the Deltans are wanton, it's because a human mating with a Deltan is not equipped to deal with that level of intimacy."

In the only canonical reference to the oath of celibacy, Ilia says, 'I would never take advantage of

"MY FAVORITE *STAR TREK* MOVIE IS STILL *THE VOYAGE HOME*, WHICH I FELT WAS ESSENTIALLY THE SAME STORY AS *STAR TREK: THE MOTION PICTURE*, ONLY DONE THE WAY IT SHOULD HAVE BEEN DONE."

Creating the Vulcan landscape

a sexually-immature species,' and Povill points out that "the difference is that Gene would call it 'sexually-immature species,' and I would call it 'emotionally-immature species.' That's the difference between Gene and me."

The team behind *Star Trek: The Motion Picture* were not invited to return to the franchise for the succeeding movies, with even Roddenberry forced into an 'Executive Consultant' role. Povill himself "was invited in to pitch a few times on *Star Trek: The Next Generation*. It was a very strange experience pitching *Next Generation*. I even pitched *Voyager* at the very beginning because I actually had some good ideas, I think."

Povill made a return to *Star Trek* when his *Phase II* script "The Child" became the basis for one of *Star Trek: The Next Generation's* early episodes – although Povill's original intentions were changed in the process.

"The A and B stories were completely severed in terms of how they worked with each other, and the emotional impact was completely blunted," Povill says. "And philosophically, the notion that the child sacrifices herself for the good of the ship and, like V'Ger, goes on to the next stage of her existence was the heart and soul of the story for me – it's

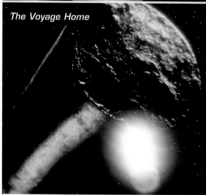

The Voyage Home

sort of analogous to a Christ story. To take out its philosophical or spiritual roots, as it were, was just to completely butcher it as far as I was concerned."

Povill lost touch with the show in its later years, revealing "I pretty much stopped watching somewhere in the middle of *The Next Generation*. I saw a few episodes of *Voyager*, I saw one or two episodes of *Enterprise*, but I had long since ceased to be a fan in the sense of seeing the show religiously. And there were features that I never saw.

"My favorite *Star Trek* movie is still The *Voyage Home*, which I felt was essentially the same story as *Star Trek: The Motion Picture*, only done the way it should have been done. I thought the spine of the story was exactly the same as ours, but it really did a vastly better job telling it than we did."▲

ROBERT WISE

Best known for his Academy Award-winning direction of the hit musicals *West Side Story* and *The Sound of Music*, Robert Earl Wise will forever be remembered by *Star Trek* fans as the first director to bring the voyages of the *U.S.S. Enterprise* to the silver screen with *Star Trek: The Motion Picture*. Other noteworthy directorial credits include the original *The Day the Earth Stood Still* (1951), *Run Silent, Run Deep* (1958), *The Haunting* (1963) and *The Andromeda Strain* (1971).

Wise's work in the film industry encompassed the roles of director, sound effects editor, producer, and film editor, and it was in that last capacity that he achieved notoriety for his work in the acclaimed 1941 Orson Welles drama, *Citizen Kane*, for which he received a Oscar nomination. In 1998, Wise was the recipient of a Lifetime Achievement Award from the American Film Institute, considered the highest career achievement honor in Hollywood. He died in 2005.

AN APPOINTMENT WITH ETERNITY

As the Nexus-addicted Dr. Tolian Soran in *Star Trek: Generations*, acting legend Malcolm McDowell played a pivotal part in *Star Trek* lore, and in the process became the most loathed villain in the history of the franchise...
Interview by Calum Waddell

Despite having done the 'bad guy' thing in numerous classic movies – including brutal teenage gang leader Alex in Stanley Kubrick's *A Clockwork Orange*, which remains his signature role – it was McDowell's character in *Generations* which proved to be the actor's most life-threatening project, when he went down in history as the man who killed Captain Kirk. In fact, he was even afforded police protection, when a very small minority of enraged *Star Trek* fans sent him death threats.

"I have been asked before if that was all just a big publicity stunt," says the actor. "But it is absolutely true. Some *Star Trek* fans just couldn't give Kirk up! It was in the infancy of the internet, so everyone thought they could get away with it. You can't really throw around threats like that today."

Interestingly, McDowell first obtained notice of the furious fan reaction via another *Star Trek* thespian. "I heard about it from my nephew, who is also an actor – Alexander Siddig," he recalls.

"He played the character of Julian Bashir on *Deep Space Nine*, and he called me to say, 'Uncle Malcolm, I have just been online and you are getting death threats from some of the fans for killing Kirk.' My first thought was, 'My God, they should be happy! What's the matter with these people?' But the studio, Paramount, took it seriously and they hired two ex-Los Angeles police officers to come to New York while we were doing our press interviews. I have to say, it was a bit embarrassing because not even one fan

"SOME *STAR TREK* FANS JUST COULDN'T GIVE KIRK UP."

Malcolm McDowell as Soran

came up and asked me for an autograph. They were clearly disgusted that I had accepted this role in the first place (*laughs*)."

Today, McDowell sees a lot of humor in his *Generations* experience. "I remember at 9pm on a Saturday night, after we had finished our press interviews, some of the cast said, 'Let's go and get a meal'," smiles the actor. "I thought that sounded good, but the police officers said, 'Well, we'd better go with you, Malcolm', which I felt was preposterous. Anyway, when we exited the hotel, I looked left and I looked right, and the street was completely deserted. Not one person was waiting outside to kill me!"

In spite of such craziness, McDowell says that he has no regrets about being involved with the *Star Trek* series. "They were all very good actors on that film," he recalls. "The cast were a well-oiled machine, and they were very welcoming to me. Each of them was extremely nice. They had been together for several years by that time, so I could have been treated as an outsider, but that was never the case. And it was a lot of fun working with Shatner. I have always enjoyed his work, and I think he is a huge presence on the screen. I think the *Star Trek* fans have a lot to thank him for, because between Shatner and Leonard Nimoy, it endured for decades. These are still the two icons of the series. "

Asked whether he was a fan of *Star Trek* before taking the role, McDowell admits that he had a distanced admiration for the franchise. "I always respected what *Star Trek* is," he says. "Each episode is a little morality tale dressed up in the science fiction genre and, of course, that's great. Gene Roddenberry was an extraordinary man, and he certainly came up with some

Malcolm McDowell prepares a scene for *Silent Night, Deadly Night*

fantastic stuff. What an imagination he had. And people still love *Star Trek* and talk about the old Shatner series, which speaks volumes. As for *Generations*, I thought that the film was rather good. I haven't seen it in a few years, but I remember thinking that it was very well done, exceptionally directed by David Carson – who is a fellow Brit – and I am very proud of it."

Conversation quickly turns to whether or not McDowell prefers to be typecast as 'the villain' – something that's become his trademark ever since the blockbuster success of *A Clockwork Orange*. "Look, villains are always great to portray," he chuckles. "In fact, usually they are the part that every actor wants to do. A movie is really only as good as its villain."

Of course, it is Stanley Kubrick's futuristic masterpiece *A Clockwork Orange* – in which McDowell portrayed the jack-booted thug Alex

DeLarge – which still defines the performer. Thanks to some brutal and disturbing sequences, *A Clockwork Orange* whipped up a storm of controversy, leading to Kubrick's decision to remove it from distribution in Britain for decades (it was finally re-released in 1999, following the director's death). The feature also gained critical acclaim and Oscar nominations for its powerful portrayal of wasted youth and a right-wing government which instigates an enforced program of painful 'mental rehabilitation,' in order to deal with teenage troublemakers.

"The youth were fighting back at that time," recalls McDowell, when asked about his part in the movie. "And I think I was in the right place at the right time. I guess my face was just punkish enough to work in the role. And, you know, I suffered to make that film. I scratched my corneas. It was in the scene where they force my

Malcolm McDowell as Soran in *Star Trek: Generations*

Soran plays with Picard's emotions in *Star Trek: Generations*

eyes open with these lid locks and make me watch all number of violent videos to try and 'rehabilitate' me. I was sat bolt upright, and my eyes were supposed to be anaesthetized, which meant I was not supposed to feel anything. However, I bloody well did feel it when the locks slipped off and tore their way down my eyeballs. That was not a nice thing at all!"

Recently, McDowell has been seen in remakes of the horror classics *Halloween* (2007) and *Silent Night, Deadly Night* (2012). Given this, how would he feel if he heard that *A Clockwork Orange* was going to be remade?

"I would say good luck to them," he insists. "It is interesting because, obviously, the political landscape has changed since the early 70s, but that is also what keeps the young people coming back to *A Clockwork Orange*. It is not the violence or the futuristic look – which is not very futuristic

"IT WAS A LOT OF FUN WORKING WITH SHATNER. I HAVE ALWAYS ENJOYED HIS WORK."

anymore, given that the film shows cassette players and everything, although I think the production design is still pretty timeless. No, what really stands out about *A Clockwork Orange* is the fact it is about 'Big Brother' taking over your life. That is probably more prevalent now than it was back when we made it. I would say government intervention in your life is way more now than it was back in 1970. From that point of view, *A Clockwork Orange* is more topical today than it was when it came out."

Another sci-fi classic that McDowell took on was *Time After Time* (1979), in which he played a time-traveling H.G. Wells who pursues Jack the Ripper to present day San Francisco. The film is a favorite of genre buffs – and of McDowell as well, albeit for different reasons.

"I met my ex-wife, Mary Steenburgen, on that film," says the actor. "I always say that I love *Time After Time* because I got two great children from it. I know the sci-fi followers adore it because it is a very charming film – it has a nice heart and soul to it. Of course, it is a very different kind of sci-fi movie from *A Clockwork Orange*. It mostly takes place in modern day San Francisco, and I loved the challenge of playing a seminal character like H.G. Wells, who was a socialist and a feminist, very ahead of the curve. Then you place him in another era, where he falls in love with this modern woman, but it scares the

WALK OF FAME

In 2012, McDowell received one of his biggest honors – something which gives the Yorkshire-born screen icon a great deal of pleasure: his very own star on the Hollywood Walk of Fame.

"I am so proud of it," he enthuses. "I had a great little reception afterwards, and it was a very nice day. A lot of good friends came out to see me, including Rob Zombie and Gary Oldman, and that just added to the thrill. Gary told me that I inspired him to be an actor. To be honest, I think that alone is quite a career achievement (*laughs*)."

Malcolm McDowell tracks down a murderous Santa Claus imposter in *Silent Night*

Malcolm McDowell
in *Silent Night*

KILLING KIRK

Even more unpopular than Kirk's death as seen in the theatrical release of *Star Trek: Generations*, was the one originally shot – in which Soran murders Kirk in cold blood, shooting the heroic Captain in the back! Preview audiences were not happy at seeing Kirk go out like some cheap punk, so a rather more heroic demise was filmed.

Kirk-killing Soran

crap out of him (*laughs*). It's a brilliant concept. I love the scene where H.G. Wells walks into a McDonalds and says, 'Ah, the famous Scottish restaurant.' So, yes, *Time After Time* would go down as one of my favorites."

More recently, McDowell played the eccentric Doctor Loomis in Rob Zombie's gore-drenched remake of *Halloween* and its 2009 sequel. Though the new *Halloween* movies received mixed reviews, McDowell's raucous performance earned him praise.

"I didn't go back and watch the original *Halloween*," he admits. "I had never seen it and my opinion was 'what's the point of looking at it now?' We were not really remaking those films anyway. Of course, the basis is the same, but when you change the actors you change quite a lot. But my main reason for avoiding those original films was because I really didn't want to be influenced by Donald Pleasence [who played Doctor Loomis in the original films]. Donald was

"WHEN I MAKE A HORROR FILM, I AM ALWAYS CAST AS THE GOOD GUY. DOES THAT NOT TELL YOU HOW UPSIDE-DOWN EVERYTHING IS?"

a great performer. I love him dearly, and I really did not want his imprint in my brain, because no matter how much I would have tried to forget about him, he would still be present. So, whatever people may think about the new *Halloween*, I never copied anything that Donald did in the older ones."

Currently, McDowell can be seen in the festive slasher *Silent Night*, another scary movie remake,

based on 1984's *Silent Night, Deadly Night*. In this outing, which is played with tongue placed firmly in cheek, the actor plays a police officer on the trail of a murderous Santa Claus imposter.

"I haven't seen it, but I have heard that the original *Silent Night, Deadly Night* is really terrible," says the actor. "From what I understand, it was done on a tiny budget – which is not to say that we had lots of money but we had enough. I mean, for what it is, this film is really good. We just wanted to scare people and make them laugh. Horror movies are always a lot of fun to do. It is magnificent to be scared in the comfort of a movie theater (*laughs*). I remember, as a kid, being terrified by the Wicked Witch in *The Wizard of Oz*, and the evil Queen in *Snow White and the Seven Dwarfs*, and I loved it. But I am the hero in *Silent Night*, so go figure. It's funny, because when I make a horror film, I am always cast as the good guy. Does that not tell you how upside-down everything is?" ▲

Soran tortures Geordi
in *Star Trek: Generations*

STAR TREK SCRAPBOOK

LIGHTS! CAMERA! ENGAGE!

With the original *Star Trek* cast heading off into semi-retirement, 1994 saw the *Next Generation* set their course for multiplex stardom. Mark Phillips takes the helm on another voyage into the trivia archives, to uncover how Picard and crew fared on the silver screen.

Kirk's cliffhanger ending

Who's the best?

Russell Evanson, of *The Wisconsin State Journal,* once suggested that friendships had been "destroyed" in arguments over who was the better *Star Trek* captain – James T. Kirk or Jean-Luc Picard. In 1994, the movie-going public would finally have a chance to decide, as both characters appeared on screen together for the first (and last) time in *Star Trek: Generations.* It turned out there was no contest – the score was a definitive tie.

The momentous nature of the event was not lost on the cast of the movie. During a quiet break during filming, Patrick Stewart took two chairs emblazoned with the names Patrick Stewart and William Shatner, carefully arranged them side by side against the jaw-dropping beauty of the Sierra Nevada mountains, and took several snapshots as evidence that two captains from different generations had truly met for the

first time. "There's an enormous sense of history about this," Stewart told Joel Engel of the *New York Times* news service.

And the movie had another trump card up its sleeve – one captain wouldn't make it to the end credits...

Generations screenwriter Ronald D. Moore confessed that Kirk, "was like a childhood hero of mine. I was physically shaking and upset when I wrote that final scene of his life." Shatner himself offered to *Knight-Ridder News,* "The practicalities were against our cast continuing to another film. We were getting raises for every movie and we were getting older." Unlike Spock's demise in *Wrath of Khan,* Shatner said Kirk's death was "irrevocable."

"They shot him down like a dog!" was the outraged cry of one fan who objected to the original ending of *Generations* shown to preview

Soran welcomes the Nexus, in *Star Trek: Generations*

audiences, which saw Kirk being phasered in the back. So poorly received was this death scene that it was re-shot at the last minute, with Kirk dying more heroically while battling the crazed Soran (Malcolm McDowell). McDowell would later chuckle to the *Miami Herald*, "It's great to be remembered for killing Captain Kirk." Bob Strauss of the *LA Daily News* found Kirk's death (after falling from a bridge), "disappointing." Shatner agreed, telling Strauss, "I would have much rather gone out with the eruption of Mount St. Helens."

During an early screening of *Generations* in Madison, Wisconsin, fans cheered, laughed and, at Kirk's death scene, sniffled with grief. The movie-goers later shared their reactions with local reporters. "There should have been more of the old *Star Trek* cast," Amy lamented. Nathan laughed when "Data got his emotion chip," while Brian said, "This *Star Trek* film is better than all of the others." "Spock should have been in it," said Don. "He and Data would have been good together." And when asked if there should be a sequel, many replied, "Make it so!"

Janet Maslin of *The New York Times* praised the pomp and spectacle of *Generations* and called Malcolm McDowell "a dandy, taunting villain," noting that "*Wrath of Kahn* and *The Voyage Home* had been the only *Trek* films to connect with fans and non-fans alike. Until now."

Brent Spiner, still "perplexed" by the cancellation of the *Next Generation* television series, was enthusiastic about further cinematic voyages. He claimed the classic *Trek* characters had explored 18 percent of the universe and the *Next Generation* TV crew explored another 15 percent, which left 67 percent of the universe for future feature film adventures.

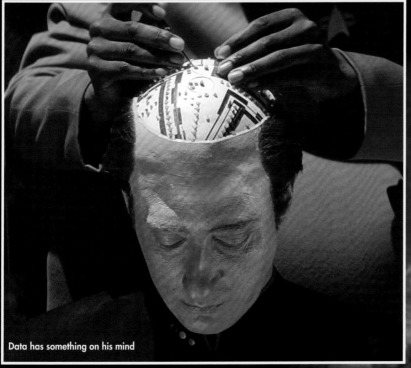

Data has something on his mind

The *Enterprise*-E battles the Borg

"Out, damned spot!"

Jonathan Frakes directs

MAKING CONTACT

Jonathan Frakes (Will Riker) had lobbied to direct a *Next Generation* film, but was surprised when the opportunity was offered to him so soon. The terrific experience of filming *First Contact* "has probably spoiled me by having this one as my maiden voyage," he said to John Lyons of *The Winnipeg Free Press*. When asked how the cast got along, he answered, "Any ego problems were done years ago... there is a wonderful frankness and respect on the set." Patrick Stewart was so impressed after screening the first ten minutes of *First Contact*, he knew they had a winner. "I am now intrigued by what we might do with this franchise," he remarked, and he envisioned 20 more years of "interesting" *Star Trek* film work ahead.

Warren Epstein of the *Springs Gazette Telegraph* called *First Contact*, "a darn good, eerie futuristic horror flick... Resistance is futile." Watching the film with an audience of fans and non-fans, Sara Voorhees of *Scripps*

Howard News Service affirmed: "This film will turn ordinary people into Trekkers." When *Voyager*'s holographic doctor (Robert Picardo) made an unexpected cameo, fans erupted into gales of surprised laughter. The cast was now firmly established as bona-fide heroes to a new generation, and Voorhees asked the actors to name their greatest hero while growing up: Families featured prominently, with Frakes nominating "my wonderful father," while others spoke about their professional heroes. Stewart cited actor Kirk Douglas, Marina Sirtis praised film star Greta Garbo, and LeVar Burton's list included Sidney Poitier. Brent Spiner said he once considered comedian Jerry Lewis "a God."

Many reviews praised Alice Krige's performance as the Borg Queen as "majestically

"ANY EGO PROBLEMS WERE DONE YEARS AGO..."
JONATHAN FRAKES

STAR TRIVIA

As a 10 year-old boy, Tom Hanks would pretend to be TV's *Batman* and do slow-motion tumbles onto his sofa, imitating the heroes of *Time Tunnel*, but he retained a special fondness for *Star Trek* and, had it not been for a scheduling conflict, Hanks was in line to play Zefram Cochrane in *Star Trek: First Contact*.

STAR TRIVIA

Scaring movie-goers out of their wits was the goal of make-up expert Michael Westmore during *First Contact*. Mission: to make the Borg look much more terrifying than they had been on TV. "We decided they would look a lot scarier with bald heads," Westmore told writer Richard Ryan about his decision to remove their helmets. Special skullcaps were created for the actors, and it took seven hours (later cut to five) to transform each actor into an unearthly movie Borg.

Frakes insists "there is no whining" on his set

evil" and "one of the most terrifying villains in science fiction history." Krige knew nothing of the *Star Trek* universe when Frakes cast her, and she immediately immersed herself in *Next Generation* episodes about the Borg. On the first day after completing her make-up, with rubber body suit and contact lenses, she heard a loud gasp from behind her. She turned around to see her startled make-up team with fear and surprise in their eyes. She knew then that her six-hour make-up transformation had succeeded. She *was* the Borg Queen!

Patrick Stewart admitted later that he had a "terrific attraction" to Alice Krige's Borg Queen "I wouldn't mind spending more time with her," he admitted to David Germain of *The Associated Press*. "She's sexy and repellent [and] has a sense of humor."

Brent Spiner (Data) and Patrick Stewart (Picard) return in *Star Trek: Insurrection*

Alice Krige as the Borg Queen

REBEL YELL

With *First Contact* judged a success on almost every level, producer Rick Berman was quoted as saying the next film had a "high concept" idea. "It is very special and it had better be," he said. "After *First Contact*, it's going to be a major job to one-up ourselves."

Frakes returned to direct *Star Trek: Insurrection* (1998), and he fondly recalled a scene where a naked Riker and Troi are in a bathtub. Frakes enjoyed watching a video playback of scenes on a nearby monitor while sitting in the water. "I didn't even have to leave the bathtub to direct," he quipped. Marina Sirtis recalled to writer David Brian Waldon that when she noticed some bubbles had evaporated, leaving her top exposed in a less-than-PG view, she looked over to Frakes,

expecting her director to show concern. Instead, all she got back from him was a big smile. The scene, of course, was re-shot – with more bubbles.

It all underlined Frakes' belief that creativity flourishes "on a fun set. There is no whining here," he noted. Even F. Murray Abraham, as guest villain Ru'afo, was impressed when the cast and crew encouraged him to share his repertoire of jokes with them during production. "The cast welcomed me without hesitation," he said. "I don't think I have ever experienced anything like that before in my career." The accomplished actor was also stunned when Frakes would burst into song at the most unexpected times. "He certainly has a wonderful baritone voice," Abraham remarked.

Shaving Riker's beard

"A British Tar..."

Special Guest Villain F. Murray Abraham, in *Star Trek: Insurrection*

"DISPENSE WITH THE HEROICS AND CONCENTRATE ON THE LAUGHS."
ROBERT W. BUTLER
OF *KNIGHT RIDDER NEWS*

During filming of *Insurrection*, *The Winnipeg Free Press* stated the *Next Generation* actors had become like family and, as LeVar Burton said, "We have this ability to crack each other up. We take it to an intense, almost perverse level." But the actor never could solve a perplexing mystery concerning his director. "Jonathan takes off his shoes while directing, which is strange," Burton observed, "I never understood that." Neither did Frakes. When confronted by a reporter over this peculiarity, he finally offered, "Maybe I need to get shoes that are more comfortable."

Before *Insurrection* premiered, Brent Spiner reflected on his good fortune to writer Patricia O'Haire. He admitted that as a working actor from 1975-87, nobody knew him. "Now people yell to me, 'Hey, Data!' and then keep going about their business. That's great!"

Insurrection (1998) was not the critical or box-office hit the previous *Next Generation* films were, but Robert W. Butler of *Knight Ridder News* called it "perfectly pleasant" for Trekkers, but seriously suggested the next film be a comedy. "Dispense with the heroics and concentrate on the laughs," he urged, partly because he was so impressed by *Insurrection*'s "deft comedy." Indeed, *The New York Daily News* noted that Spiner had an extra bounce in his step because Data had been given the emotion chip. "I can now smile as Data and do so many other things," Spiner raved about the android's new sense of humor. Hal Silliman of *The Mountain Democrat* liked most of the film's humor too, save for one early scene that made him

STAR TRIVIA

Make it... No. That was the final word when it came to depicting Picard's romance in *Insurrection*. According to Cindy Pearlman of the *Chicago Sun-Times*, Patrick Stewart's "two big kissing scenes" were cut from the film. Stewart had looked forward to showing a vulnerable side to his character by romancing a "350-year-old" beauty played by Donna Murphy, and said he was "kicking and screaming" over the executive decision to delete the kisses.

A grisly end for the Romulan Senate, in *Star Trek: Nemesis*

squirm – Picard's rendition of Gilbert and Sullivan's musical number "A British Tar".

INTO THE SUNSET

Before the final *Next Generation* film, *Nemesis* (2002) premiered, Patrick Stewart recalled to Barry Koltnow how everyone, from his agent to some actors, told him in 1987 how *The Next Generation* wouldn't last more than a year. In fact, Stewart told Joey Berlin of *Copley News Service* that "an extremely distinguished British actor" told Stewart not to take the role of Picard, that it would "wreck" his career. Stewart was glad he

Double the Data

Riker takes aim

didn't take that advice and said that now, "I don't quite know where Patrick Stewart ends and Jean-Luc Picard leaves off."

Stewart also recalled an early appearance in Denver, where he stepped on stage and was greeted by 3000 screaming fans. "I learned that day how to be more outwardly enthusiastic about the show," he said. He also got a chuckle when a scientist came up to him and said there was a crater on the moon named Picard. Stewart was happy when *X-Men* director Bryan Singer stopped by the starship set for a visit, but had a feeling during the filming of *Nemesis* that this could be his last *Trek* adventure. During rehearsals, Stewart was suddenly overcome with emotion and rendered speechless after Frakes said the line, "Serving with you has been an honor."

The financial returns for *Nemesis* were modest, and critically the film didn't assimilate the critics. Ron Weiskind always preferred *The Next Generation* over classic *Trek*, but after seeing *Nemesis* he concluded that, "the big screen is more suited to Captain Kirk's swashbuckling." Tom Di Giurco of *The Mountain Democrat* found it "highly enjoyable," with one of the most "action-packed and spectacular" space battles ever seen. Jon Niccum praised Tom Hardy as a "great new villain" (Hardy had won the role over 900 other actors) and pointed out that Stewart was responsible for much of *Trek*'s continued success. Meanwhile, *The Orange Leader* lamented that *Nemesis* valued "brawn over brains."

Perhaps the last word should go to Elizabeth Brixey, who said in *The Wisconsin State Journal* that when it came to *Star Trek*, past, present or future, it didn't *really* matter what the critics thought. Engage! ⋀

VISION QUEST

When *Star Trek* made the jump from television to cinema in 1979, the effects world had undergone a revolution. Douglas Smith and Michael Fink were part of the team tasked with making the final frontier look more astonishing than ever before. *Star Trek* Magazine spoke to the Academy Award winners about how they re-energized visual effects for *Star Trek: The Motion Picture*.

By Calum Waddell

"I got my start in the film industry by accident," says Michael Fink of his first break into movie visual effects. "I was an artist working in Los Angeles and I had a job at CalArts – the California Institute of the Arts. Now that is one of the most prestigious art schools in California, and I had a friend there who quit and went off to work in the film business. They would work on a film for six months, make a bit of money, and then they would go and work on their own art projects for the rest of the year. Of course, I thought that was a great plan (*laughs*)."

Today, Fink is widely regarded as one of the top visual effects artisans in Hollywood, with mega-budget blockbusters such as *Avatar* (2009), *TRON Legacy* (2010) and *The Tree of Life* (2011) regularly calling on his expertise. At the 2008 Academy Awards, he was honored with an Oscar for his work on *The Golden Compass* (on which he also served as a second-unit director), although Fink's early days in the film industry clearly indicated his was a talent to be taken seriously.

Taking inspiration from his artist friends, Fink quit his job and looked for an opening into the Hollywood studio system. His first few movie credits landed him knee deep in a special-effects world which, following the success of *Star Wars* in 1977, was fast-changing. These initial projects include 1979's franchise-defining *Star Trek: The Motion Picture*, on which he is credited for 'effects props and miniatures'.

"Just through sheer luck, and quite a lot of determination, I finally got asked to work on a film called *The China Syndrome*," he reveals. "That came just before *Star Trek*, and I was credited as an 'electrical consultant' on the movie. Basically, I was wiring-up lightbulbs and things like that, although I actually had no idea what I was doing (*laughs*). All I *did* know is that I liked being on a film set a lot: *The China Syndrome* was great fun. It was done on schedule and on budget, and the actors and the director were all wonderful. The producers were great too, and everyone had a really good time. It was really enjoyable and I thought, 'Wow, this is how they make movies: everyone is friendly to one another.' Of course I was completely wrong (*laughs*). In fact, I have never been on a movie set as well organized as *The China Syndrome* since then. It was a case of complete beginner's luck!"

> ## "*STAR WARS* WAS ON EVERYONE'S MIND AND WE HAD TO MAKE SURE WE COULD PRESENT SOMETHING DIFFERENT."
> ### MICHAEL FINK

Working on *Star Trek: The Motion Picture* gave Fink a meatier role in the film-making process. "I got to work with Doug Trumbull on *Star Trek*," he states. "He was the reason I got to be on that movie, and he was fantastic to be around. I was really fortunate because, beginning with *Star Trek*, I slowly moved up the ladder and got asked to do more complex things. Instead of working on lightbulbs and stuff, I was now getting to work with miniatures and I was learning from Trumbull, who pointed out how important the photography of these things are if they are to be presented with any believability in the final film. I recall learning about how to light the miniature effects carefully in order to provide a really good depth of field. Although it

was only my second job, I felt that I was given a lot of trust and things to do on *Star Trek*, which was great."

Although Fink was still relatively young when he began work on *Star Trek*, he believes it was the people skills he'd gained before breaking into the movie business that increased his responsibility on the film.

"When I did *Star Trek*, I was already 33 years old," he relates. "By that time, I had been an officer in the US army and I had done a lot of other jobs too – for instance, I had been an investment banker in San Francisco where I had a small team which I [was] in charge of – so when *Star Trek* came along, I was a fairly capable manager of people. I think that got noticed by Doug and he put a little more trust in me. We had some really good effects talent on that show too, guys like John Dykstra and Richard E. Hollander. The best directors know how to put together a great crew, and you really have to give credit to Robert Wise for hiring Doug Trumbull and his guys to work on *Star Trek*. We wanted the effects on *Star Trek* to be unique, but *Star Wars* was on everyone's mind and we had to make sure we could present something different. The end result is a great-looking movie."

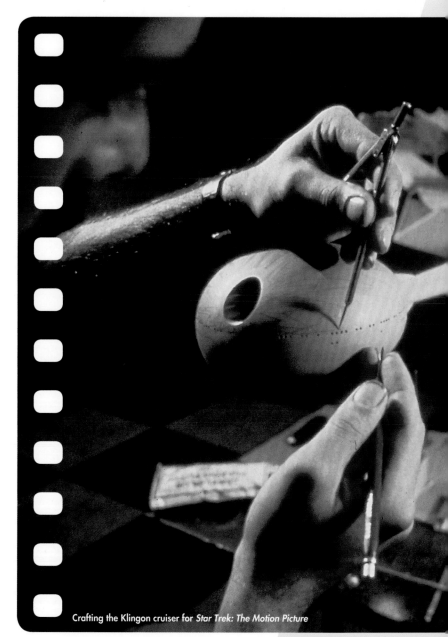

Crafting the Klingon cruiser for *Star Trek: The Motion Picture*

GALACTIC CONFLICT

Ironically, many of the team brought onboard to create the new *Trek*'s effects were veterans of George Lucas' game-changing feature, including Douglas Smith, credited with helming the 'photographic effects camera' on *The Motion Picture*, who would go on to win an Academy Award for his work on *Independence Day* (1996).

At the time, Smith was working under the tutelage of John Dykstra on the original *Star Wars* (1977), and followed the effects legend

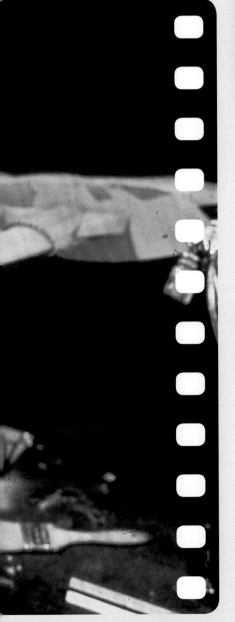

The heart of V'Ger revealed

onto *Star Trek: The Motion Picture*. According to Smith, the original *Enterprise* outing proved to be a monumental undertaking.

"*Star Trek* is an entire world unto itself," he laughs. "And that first movie had some very grand ideas. Originally, the director, Robert Wise, planned to film it on 65mm, to really give it that grand scale. In the end that did not happen, although some of the visual effects work was shot on the 65mm format which, without wishing to get too technical, allowed us to distort the scale of the spaceships and so forth. We worked with Bernie Abramson, who was a revolutionary Director of Photography, and he did some great work, especially in capturing the flow and movement of *V'Ger*, which was probably the biggest challenge we faced on *Star Trek*. We spent weeks and weeks trying to get that to work the way we wanted it to. Nowadays it would be created with computer effects."

Originally, Smith was not expecting to be doing much on *The Motion Picture* but, to his surprise, he ended up working for several weeks on the movie.

"At first we were only going to be doing some digital effects work on *Star Trek*," he reveals. "But Paramount, for whatever reason, became unhappy with some of the work that was being done on the visual effects, and they opted to get rid of the person in charge. After that, they asked Douglas Trumbull to

finish everything. Now, from what I remember, Douglas cut the visual effects work between John Dykstra and himself. I ended up photographing a lot of the Klingon warships, and making them work against the background and look as if they were actually traveling through space. I also spent some time doing *V'Ger*, and that took a long time to get right. We wanted it to be as believable and real as possible, but that was no easy task. *Star Trek* was an around the clock, heavy-duty operation for us. There was a lot of work to be done and Paramount wanted something that would look even more immediate than *Star Wars*."

"It was a big learning process for me," Smith admits. "There was definitely similarity in the processes that we used between *Star Wars* and *Star Trek*. We used a lot of remote control photography on both of those movies, and we photographed a very deep depth of field which allowed us to superimpose the visual effects over this tremendous scale of film. But there were some differences as well, especially the style of lighting. The lighting in *Star Trek* is very different from *Star Wars*. I think what we did in *Star Trek* is far moodier. The style was different as well, it was shot differently and I think it looked more epic. Douglas Trumbull wanted some ambient lighting too, especially inside the *Enterprise*, and that was a challenge. I am not sure we got it quite right actually (*laughs*)."

V'ger merges with Decker

exercise a lot more caution than he does now. He got a lot of the American crew fairly upset: 'Who does this guy think he is?' So, yes, there were a lot of issues going on with that movie. As for me, I was originally hired to work on the interiors of the cars, but I got thrust into a whole lot of other things after that. I was basically an art director on *Blade Runner,* but I was not in the union so I couldn't be given that title on the credits. So they called me 'action props supervisor.'"

Tales of rundown cast and crew members on *Blade Runner* have become the stuff of movie

> ## "STAR TREK WAS AN AROUND THE CLOCK, HEAVY-DUTY OPERATION FOR US."
> ### DOUGLAS SMITH

Decker and Kirk

CHANGING TIMES

Following *Star Trek: The Motion Picture*, both Smith and Fink would find themselves working on movies destined to become revered sci-fi classics.

Douglas Smith moved onto Tobe Hooper's mega-budgeted flop *Lifeforce* (1984), Mel Brooks' *Star Wars* spoof *Spaceballs* (1987), and the sci-fi comedy *My Stepmother is an Alien* (1988).

"I worked with John Dykstra again on *Lifeforce*," Smith affirms. "We actually used many of the same visual effects tricks that we did on *Star Trek* for that movie. You know, in a lot of ways I was very lucky because I was working in the early stages of digital effects. A lot of the filmmakers that established themselves in their careers during that time, or who followed *Star Wars* and *Star Trek*, later came to me and asked me to come onboard, which was fantastic."

For Fink, it was Ridley Scott's 1982 futuristic-noir *Blade Runner* (as 'action prop supervisor'), and as 'special visual effects supervisor' on 1984's eccentrically charming *The Adventures of Buckaroo Banzai Across the 8th Dimension*.

"*Blade Runner* is the only movie I have ever worked on where watching it was the same feeling I had when I was making it," laughs Fink. "I was out there on these neon-lit streets, with the rain flowing, and it was long nights, [with] crowds and crowds of extras walking by and poor Ridley Scott trying to get everyone to cooperate and everything to function in the soaking wet. We were all immersed in that futuristic sci-fi world. However, I found working for Ridley to be really exciting. I loved *Alien* and knew he was a great filmmaker, but there were other people on the set who weren't having such a good time. I think at that point in his career he had to

legend, and Fink cheerfully confirms that this is more or less how it was.

"Oh yeah, the hours were brutal on *Blade Runner*," he reflects. "On one occasion I worked for an entire stretch of nine days. I spent each day and night on the set. I didn't even have the chance to go home. At the end of it, I was hallucinating and I couldn't think straight *(laughs)*, but Ridley was very happy with my work and I am so proud that I got to work on his movie. I learned more from being on *Blade Runner* than from being on anything else."

"There were a lot of long hours on something like *Star Trek*," says Fink. "But it was also a more graceful pace back then. The directors had to live with their movies for longer. If they wanted something to be changed it took a lot of time to arrange that. Digital effects make changing [shots] quicker now. In 1979, scenes were not cut as fast as they are today either. When you were on something like *Star Trek*, it was a very long adventure until the end." ▲

Enterprise retooled

DIGITAL BLOB

When asked to name one of his greatest challenges, Fink looks back to the days of practical wizardry and his involvement in the 1988 remake of B-movie classic *The Blob*.

"I recall they talked to me about supervizing *The Blob*, and at first I had no intention of doing it," states Fink. "I really didn't understand why anyone wanted to do a remake of *The Blob* anyway *(laughs)*. I said to the director, Chuck Russell, 'Is it still going to be the same blob?' Chuck said, 'It's going to have tentacles, but that's about it.' I said 'But no eyes, right?' He said, 'Nope, no eyes.' So I thought they had the same problem that the original had, which is: 'how do you sell an audience on a monster that has no expression?'

Anyway, I turned it down but they had real problems with the film and they came back to me. So I went in and I charged them what seemed like a King's ransom at the time *(laughs)*. I more or less just stirred the pot a bit, spent a lot of money and got the monster to at least seem believable." Interestingly enough, at the time they wanted to create *The Blob* with CG, which was unthinkable in 1988."

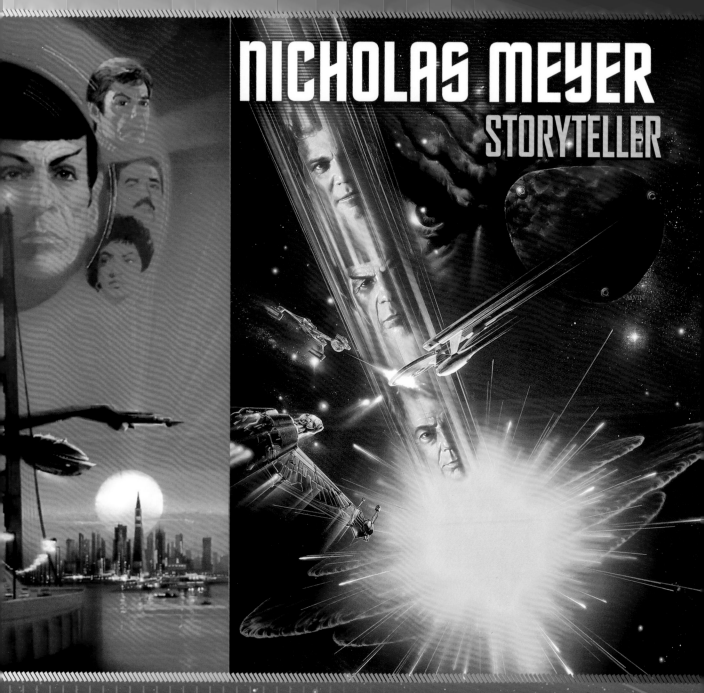

NICHOLAS MEYER
STORYTELLER

Nicholas Meyer enjoys telling stories, as anyone who's read his recent autobiography *The View From The Bridge* will know. The famed writer and director of *Star Trek II: The Wrath of Khan* and *Star Trek VI: The Undiscovered Country*, and co-writer of *Star Trek IV: The Voyage Home*, cut his directorial teeth on the H.G. Wells vs. Jack the Ripper tale *Time After Time*, before being brought on board by Harve Bennett for *The Wrath of Khan*. His TV movie *The Day After* was the most watched in American TV history, and he continues to write and direct. Over a long lunch in Los Angeles, he reminisced about his time in the 23rd Century.

Star Trek Magazine: **When you were presented with the five different script versions of *Star Trek II*, was there any stage where you thought, "This could work with a few changes," or were you always cherry picking sections?**

Nicholas Meyer: You are talking about events that happened many years ago and one has to resist the temptation, even an unconscious temptation, to engage in mythopoesis. To the best of my recollection, I was not taken with any of these drafts. I do not think I would have gone to the place I went if I had seen possibilities. Nobody said anything to me – they had all basically thrown in the towel. And that is not illusory. It was done.

Why did you reuse Khan, rather than create someone fresh?

You have to understand something about me temperamentally, and also in a way about Harve Bennett. I love recycling. I'm very big on older buildings that get redecorated: Ghirardelli Square and The Cannery in San Francisco won big architectural awards when they were refurbished. Also, you have to couple this with my abysmal ignorance of the world of *Star Trek*...

> ## "I DID KNOW AS I WAS WATCHING MONTALBAN IN HIS FIRST SCENES IN THE CARGO BAY THAT I WAS WATCHING A VERY GREAT ACTOR... I REMEMBER THINKING, AS I WATCHED HIM AND HE WAS BREAKING MY HEART, THAT HE SHOULD PLAY LEAR."

Which was an advantage coming in at that stage?

It may have been, but whether it was an advantage or a disadvantage, it was a reality. And the reality was I didn't even begin to know what the possibilities for villains was in this show. The kind of artist I am, I'm better at being a rag picker and a pillager of other people's notions and ideas and saying, "This is awfully good but...." Handel was once accused of stealing someone's tune and he said, "Yes, I stole it – that idiot didn't know what to do with it and I showed him." I'm not about to call anybody an idiot, but I think that Khan was ready-made.

Also, Harve Bennett, who I think in the book I credit with a very analytical temperament, a very analytical cast of mind which I do not possess, said, "This is a very good idea for a villain. He's one dropped shoe – they left him some place. What's going on? The actor's still alive."

Ricardo Montalban as Khan

A deadly feud in space

Had they approached Ricardo Montalban at that stage?

They hadn't approached anybody, because we didn't know what we were doing! They had nothing. The first time I ever met Bennett, he said, "Draft five is coming in," so I went home and thought, "Great, they'll send me draft five." Then I woke up and it was something like three weeks later and I never heard from him. I called up and said, "What happened?" At which point he gave me his famous "My tit's in a wringer" line. With the moribund arrival of draft five, the project was essentially dead. I speculate in the book that it was entirely possible, given how studios then worked – I don't know if that's how they work now, because all bets seem to be off – that they would have regrouped, gone on to another draft with another writer and tried again. It would have taken them another year, or whatever...

Was the world screaming for a second *Star Trek* movie at that point?

The funny thing is, the studio thought it was. They weren't wrong. I don't know what they would have done, or when they would have done it. But the fact that the first movie was a runaway production but nonetheless had made a substantial amount of money, convinced them that even if they did it in a way that was then considered wrong, people would come out. They were very intent on trying to make another one, because they did believe there was a market; they just didn't want to spend $45 million!

Ricardo Montalban dominates the screen as Khan – did you ever regret that there wasn't a physical confrontation between Khan and Kirk in the movie?
No. I never gave it a thought. I know that Bill Shatner did. I thought it was cheesy. I can point to a number of films, and a number of real-life events, in which the protagonist and the antagonist never meet. It did not concern me much. I guess I thought that that kind of confrontation with these two people, being gladiators, would be cheesy, stereotyped and familiar.

If there's a regret that I have – which I didn't have for the first 20 years and then somebody pointed it out to me, and I thought, "There's an interesting missed moment" – it's that Khan never sees Kirk get away.

He goes to his death believing that he has succeeded. I wonder, if I'd thought of it, would I have? I have some ambivalence about taking it away from him, but it's very interesting that we didn't even think of it. You play that moment earlier when he realizes that there is no override, and they can't do anything about raising the shields. That look of consternation – how different would that have been from his look at the end? Other than the man who goes to his death believing that he's avenged his wife.

When you were prepping *The Wrath of Khan* did you watch submarine movies?
You bet! I looked at *The Enemy Below* a lot. Robert Mitchum vs Curt Jurgens – that's a great flick. I looked at *Run Silent, Run Deep*.

For things to do, or things to avoid?
Things to do. These were movies that I loved and I wanted to see how they did it.

What about Khan's original appearance in "Space Seed"?
Yes. That was also part of what had intrigued Harve and then he showed it to me. That was the first time that I went, "He's a cool character," So mysterious. For so much of it you didn't know what the hell was going on with that guy, but you knew it wasn't good.

Khan has become the gold standard for *Star Trek* movie villains. Did you have any idea that he would resonate for so long?
Truthfully I can't say that I predicted anything like his preeminence, or anything like the stature which has been accorded this movie as a total construct. Never.

Khan gets angry

Saavik and Spock

U.S.S. RELI

Kirk and son

I did know as I was watching Montalban in his first scenes in the cargo bay that I was watching a very great actor, and I had had no idea. I remember thinking, as I watched him and he was breaking my heart, that he should play Lear. He made some self-deprecating comment about his accent, which I remember thinking was completely irrelevant. Notwithstanding any Hispanic inflection, his enunciation, his articulation was perfect. That's as close as I came to realizing that Khan had a kind of Lear-like grandeur when played by this guy. The arrogance and the pain walked hand in hand.

Montalban was not typically an angry guy, not, as some actors, a "squawky bird." He was a gentleman of a rather old-school cut. Humorous, generous, very smart in a kind of intuitive way.

Did you expect to be able to do one master shot of the cargo bay scene when you wrote it?
I don't think I was thinking of about how to shoot it when I wrote it. When I was finished and looked at it, I thought it would be fun to do in one – and we did. I knew I'd break it up, because we needed reaction shots, but I just thought, "What fun to let the actor work up his own head of steam." Little did I know what his first pass at that was going to entail – his voice reverberating among the rafters!

> "HANDEL WAS ONCE ACCUSED OF STEALING SOMEONE'S TUNE AND HE SAID, "YES, I STOLE IT – THAT IDIOT DIDN'T KNOW WHAT TO DO WITH IT AND I SHOWED HIM." I'M NOT ABOUT TO CALL ANYBODY AN IDIOT, BUT I THINK THAT KHAN WAS READY-MADE."

Was there ever any pressure exerted by the studio over the changes you wanted to make to the look and feel of _Star Trek_?
I recently was back at my alma mater, the University of Iowa, where my papers are stored, and they had a big, very fancy exhibit of some of this material which I had completely forgotten about. I saw memos that I had written in passionate defense of decisions that had been made by me.

I thought I had shaken hands with Gene Roddenberry and that was it, but obviously, whether it was to my face or not, there had been a good deal of harrumphing on his part, even then. I just saw that they always insisted that Starfleet was a non-military organization – they would go so far as to say it was like the Coast Guard. I would say, "Even in the Coast Guard, they call women officers Mister." I obviously was on the defensive even then, trying to preserve what I was after.

I think it's fair to say the studio has always been cynically indifferent one way or the other. "Is the picture going to make money? Is it going to come in on budget? Don't talk to us about the _Star Trek_ world!" In that capacity, I think they saw Gene at the time as a contractual, necessary evil.

Evidently, there were battles about what I was doing. They weren't battles with the studio. I did hear latterly, I don't remember where from, but the whole bruiting about that the movie was about, or involved

STAR TREK IV: THE VOYAGE HOME

In the book, you explain that for _Star Trek IV_, Harve Bennett wrote the opening and closing acts while you wrote the second and third. Were you writing simultaneously?
Yes, because it was very last minute when we came on. There was no time. It was also a tribute to what a well-oiled machine we were at that point. I think it was just put together.

I thought it was so funny that I was being asked to do a second time-travel movie in San Francisco!

Did you know the city well?
When I drove west to seek my fortune, I had an aunt who lived there, so I went and stayed with her for a month. I put all the things I loved in _Time After Time_, all those locations.

There's not a lot of San Francisco being San Francisco in _The Voyage Home_?
Every time we depict San Francisco in the 23rd Century, we're still somehow depicting the Golden Gate Bridge. In _Star Trek II_, you see San Francisco in the 23rd Century from Kirk's apartment. In _Star Trek IV_ and _Time After Time_, San Francisco is playing itself, which does make it easier.

Would you have altered the basic beats if you'd decided to set it in, say, Paris?
That's an interesting question – we never even got as far as considering that problem. In that regard, where the whales are living when they get there makes a lot of sense. There are a couple of superb aquariums in Monterey, which is just down the coast, so you can buy into that. Maybe it wouldn't have been whales... "These rabbits are of crucial importance!"

Unlike your other two _Star Trek_ movies, there's no central villain in _Star Trek IV_. Was this a conscious choice?
There _is_ a villain in _IV_, the greatest villain of all the _Treks_ – and other places besides. He is never named.

Spock and Kirk visit
20th Century San Francisco

The Undiscovered Country

Sulu (George Takei) gets a promotion

Christopher Plummer as Chang

the death of Spock, was something that had been released from his camp as a way of making trouble – which it did.

In the book, you describe your meeting with Gene Roddenberry where you told him your plans for Star Trek VI, and you say that you mishandled him, leading to an argument you regret. How do you think you should have played it?
That's a very interesting question! How should I have? There's a line in *My Fair Lady* where Rex Harrison is saying you should never let a woman in your life.

"She will beg you for advice / Your reply will be concise / And she will listen very nicely / Then go out and do exactly what she wants."

I think that's what I should have done. I should have listened, and not engaged him in debate. I think that was tactless and pointless. It was stupid. Somewhere I was so enthusiastic about the script at that point – so pleased with what it was and how to my way of thinking, it was original and different and ratcheting up things and taking these people seriously as human beings, complete with prejudices and foibles – and there was this man saying, "No, no, no the perfectability of man..." I'm thinking, where's the evidence of the perfectability of man? It was the wrong moment to take up cudgels. Just stupid.

Both Khan and Chang are charismatic men, both think they're right. Did you think of them as villains or antagonists?
Antagonists – in Aristotelian terms, they are definitely antagonists. They are "second actors." I also was intent on differentiating them psychologically. Khan's story is intensely personal. He was abandoned, his wife died as a result of the abandonment. He is seeking revenge. This is all heart.

Chang is all head. He is a creature, understandably, of realpolitik. He is Bismarck to Gorkon's Kaiser Bill – although there's something very Lincoln-esque about

Gorkon and we kept trying to emphasize that physically. All these analogies break down sooner or later!

Chang is a cold warrior for whom battle, combat, victory are heady concepts, rather than emotional. I think I described him as having a merry smile and a heart of lead. Shakespeare-spouting – "We have heard the chimes at midnight."

Did you consciously write Chang as an antithesis to Khan?
Yes. I wanted a very different villain. At the end of the day, because it's head and not heart, he may not have crawled into the affections of people in the same way as Khan.

I think Chang is a really good villain: I have a soft spot for him. I worked backwards into him. Way before I was writing this, I had acquired the Chandos CD of Christopher Plummer reciting *Henry V* to William Walton's film score from the Laurence Olivier movie. It's an amazing CD. I used to sit around blasting this thing and listening to that trumpet voice. It's the only time, barring creating a *Star Trek* movie that involves a cast of pre-existing characters, that I ever wrote a movie with an actor I didn't have, saying "If I don't get this actor, I'm screwed, because no-one else can do this. It won't be the same." I said to Mary Jo Slater, "Bring him back alive. I know we only have two nickels but you have to do this."

> ## "CHANG IS MERRY IN A MIRTHLESS WAY. YES IT WAS DELIBERATE IN CONTRAST TO KHAN WHOSE HEART IS ON HIS SLEEVE."

Did he need persuading?
I don't know any of the details. He just said, "Please don't bury me under a load of makeup so I can't act." I had a delightful time with it. He also happens to be a music fool, so we spent our time talking about Polish composers that no one ever heard of!

Did you ever have to rein him in?
Interestingly enough, no. He was almost the opposite of Montalban, who needed a lot of direction and knew he needed it. Plummer knows basically that he's a stage actor and that his outsized aura has a really rough time in movies. He's always got to make

smaller, smaller, smaller... and when you look at him in movies, you can always witness that almost sort of weird tension of an actor tamping himself down to try to fit into the camera.

On the other hand, if you are in a movie where this character is constantly declaiming Shakespeare, it's hard to say, "Cry havoc and let slip the dogs of war" in a mumble! Chang is merry in a mirthless way. Yes, it was deliberate in contrast to Khan whose heart is on his sleeve.

Both films have been released on DVD with some extra footage...
I wouldn't let them call them Director's Cuts in my case, because the addition of arguably 60 seconds of additional footage to clarify a couple of plot points that I lost battles on with the studio doesn't really constitute calling it that.

The only Director's Cut of a movie where I really thought, "This is significantly different," is the Walter Murch transcription of Orson Welles' notes for *Touch of Evil*. They're always longer but I don't think they're necessarily better. ▲

DON'T TELL ME! YOU'RE FROM OUTER SPACE

STAR DATE: 1986.
HOW ON EARTH CAN THEY SAVE THE FUTURE?

STAR TREK IV
THE VOYAGE HOME

She may be better recognized these days for playing *7th Heaven's* stalwart matriarch Annie Camden, but for *Star Trek* fans, *Catherine Hicks* will always be known as the girl who knocked back James T. Kirk, in *Star Trek IV: The Voyage Home.*

Interview by Ian Spelling
Additional Material by Pat Jankiewicz

"It's *7th Heaven*, more than anything else – by a longshot!" Catherine Hicks declares, when asked which role she is most recognized for. Aaron Spelling's family drama ran from 1996 to 2006, and starred Hicks as hard-pressed mom Annie Camden, recognized in 2009 as one of the top 10 TV moms in television history. "It's still *7th Heaven*, even now, and it doesn't surprise me at all. If you're in people's homes every week for 11 years, you're in the family. After that, it's probably *Star Trek*. I'm probably still recognized five times a day for *The Voyage Home*. When the movie came out, I was swarmed. It was constant swarmings of people.

It's not every girl that turns down James Tiberius Kirk!

CHEERLEADING

Hicks was born in New York City and grew up in Scottsdale, Arizona. "In the '50s, there was nothing there, nothing at all, but Navajo Indians, cowboys, and my parents," says Hicks, "I think it was very lonely for me. It made me love people and want to be around a lot of them, so I always wanted to be in front of people. I didn't know about theater or acting in high school or college, so I became a cheerleader."

"When I went to Notre Dame *(the university, not the Parisian cathedral, so no tenuous hunchback links there! – Ed.)*, I wanted to be a Notre Dame cheerleader out on the field during an exciting football game. I missed getting it by one vote, so I was very depressed," she recalls, "I passed the theater building and saw how happy the theater majors were. One Saturday night, on the way to a beer party at Notre Dame, I stopped in and they were doing *OLIVER!* I thought, 'These kids on a Saturday night are really doing something with their time, and I want to be like them!'
Pat Jankiewicz

"I'M PROBABLY STILL RECOGNIZED FIVE TIMES A DAY FOR *THE VOYAGE HOME*."

Catherine Hicks as Dr. Gillian Taylor

It was flattering and touching, but also, for my daughter, it was hard. I didn't want her to be in my shadow in any way."

"In normal life, people say, 'Oh, what a darling girl you are,'" Hicks continues, "but in her life it's sometimes been, 'Where's your mom?' That sometimes took the fun out of it for me. So that could be intrusive, but any actor wants to be recognized – that's why you go into it! And if you don't want to be bothered by the paparazzi, you don't go to places where you know they'll be."

Hicks is a straight shooter. Ask her a question and she'll give you a candid answer. Case in point, she openly admits having known

"Transporter, thanks!" Hicks says, laughing at herself. "I thought it was some big Christmas tree. Leonard Nimoy said, 'No, no. You don't look up and go, Aaah. It's a little thing,' and he pulled one out of his desk drawer. And I went, 'Oh, OK.'"

Actually, Hicks must mean… a communicator.

"Yes, a communicator!" she says, as a thought dawns on her, "That's why the audience didn't get what I was talking about in my talk the other day. I said 'transformer' or 'transporter' instead of 'communicator'! When we were doing the movie, before we'd beam up, I'd said to Bill [Shatner] and Leonard, 'Beaming

"I THOUGHT I WOULD USE THE IGNORANCE FOR THE CHARACTER, BECAUSE SHE REALLY WAS *ALICE IN WONDERLAND*."

He's from Iowa. He only works in outer space

nothing at all about *Star Trek* when she landed the role of Dr. Gillian Taylor, whale-loving assistant director of the Cetacean Institute, who helps Captain Kirk, Spock and the crew of the *U.S.S. Enterprise* save the day in *Star Trek IV: The Voyage Home*.

"I didn't know anything about *Star Trek*," she says. "That wasn't intentional. I missed it. I was out in the front yard, looking at the house across the street that belonged to the boy I had a crush on. I just missed *Star Trek*. So, at the audition, I didn't even know what a transformer was…"

Um… transporter?

up, what does it mean? What does it feel like.' They'd say, 'It tingles.' But that unfamiliarity played to the character, and when I got the role I purposely did not educate myself by watching all the previous stuff. I thought I would use the ignorance for the character, because she really was *Alice in Wonderland*, and that's what I did."

TANKED

Hicks shot *The Voyage Home* nearly 30 years ago now. However, her recollections of the experience remain vivid. She speaks warmly of the "kindness and friendliness" of the main cast – particularly Leonard Nimoy, who was

WORKING CLOSE-UP

The role of biologist Dr. Taylor was originally written with comedian Eddie Murphy in mind, before morphing into the reluctant object of desire for one James Tiberius Kirk. "Well, William Shatner was so funny and witty, you couldn't help but laugh. Sometimes, he would come to my trailer and I didn't know what he was saying," says Hicks with a playful grin. "I also found that with him, I sort of learned that I had to fight for my coverage and close-ups. He started saying to Nimoy, 'Leonard, you'll want to shoot it this way…' I went to Leonard's house one Sunday morning while we were filming the movie, wrote him a long letter and dropped it off. Leonard said 'Come on in!' I did, and he told me, 'We've worked together a long time, Bill and I, and it will all be fine'. And he was right, it was. It really was. I am still glad I fought for one particular close-up, though."

What close-up was that? "It was at the aquarium, when I run up, mad at Mr. Spock for swimming with the whales. I said to Leonard, 'This should be my shot alone, talking to both Kirk and Spock together in a two-shot, because it's my whales and my scene.' He agreed. Leonard did it that way, and it's a great shot!"

"I am really proud of my *Star Trek* movie; I love it. I think it's very funny and charming. I especially love when I say to Shatner, 'Don't tell me! You're from outer space,' and he responds, 'No, I'm from Iowa. I only work in outer space.' How can you not love that?"

At the finale, she even rejects James T. Kirk when he puts the moves on her. "Yeah, that final scene was fun to film. It was my idea to kiss him goodbye because I felt we had gone through a lot together, and probably care a lot for each other by that point. I didn't know the history of Captain Kirk's famous romances. I was just playing it from my point of view, which was 'I hope to see you again, but I'm NOT gonna hook up with you!'"
Pat Jankiewicz

WHALE WATCHING

Gillian Taylor is a whale expert, caring for George and Gracie – two humpback whales that Kirk needs to bring back to a 23rd Century where the great mammals are long extinct, in order to save the planet Earth. Because she has no family or significant ties to her own time, Gillian joins her whales in the future to oversee the humpbacks' care and the species' re-population.

"To prepare myself for it, I would go to the ocean and look out at the waves and think about whales," Hicks says happily. "Working with the whales proved no challenge at all, because I never saw them! The whales were all shot later and added into the window of the aquarium, so I never actually saw them, but I just imagined them."

Saving imaginary whales had a positive effect on her real life. "I got involved with Greenpeace because of the movie, and it made me want to get involved with the whole 'Save the Whales' cause. I am sad to say they are back to killing whales now, Japan and Norway, and several other countries."

Pat Jankiewicz

pulling double duty, playing Spock and directing the film – and reveals that they treated her like "their little princess." It could, she points out, have gone in an entirely different direction. "I had a big role," she explains. "Some actors could be threatened or bitchy or mean. Bill was fun, a bit competitive, but I fought for my shots with Leonard. Leonard did not yet know he was a brilliant director, and the reviews of our film launched him into the mainstream. I don't remember a struggle at all. I just remember fun, fun, fun."

One scene in particular impressed the cast and crew as much as it would impress audiences – the climactic sequence in which the stricken Klingon *Bird-of-Prey* is submerged in San Francisco Bay, and our heroes fight to stay afloat. Shot on the parking lot/water tank at Paramount Pictures, Nimoy marshaled every trick in the book to pull it off. The capacity-filled tank, a partially submerged *Bird-of-Prey* prop and fake whale tail, were surrounded by rigging and decks for the cameras. Up high, crewmen operated wind machines that whipped water onto the actors below, and lightning machines produced loud, frightful crackling. It was epic filmmaking of the old school, and Hicks loved every moment.

Gillian heads back to the future

"That was so neat, that whole tank sequence," remembers Hicks, "I'd been in New York, on Broadway with Jack Lemmon. You get wooed by agents and you come out, and they pick you up at the airport. I got a series right away called *The Bad News Bears*, with Jack Warden. I was staying in Beverly Hills, at a hotel, and I'd rent a car and drive on Melrose to Paramount Studios, and I parked in this sunken, recessed section of the parking lot. So you'd drive down into it and park, and I was like, 'What is that?' And there was huge blue sky scrim behind it. I'd always think, 'Oh, isn't that neat?'

"Cut to years later, and I arrive at Paramount to work on *The Voyage Home*,

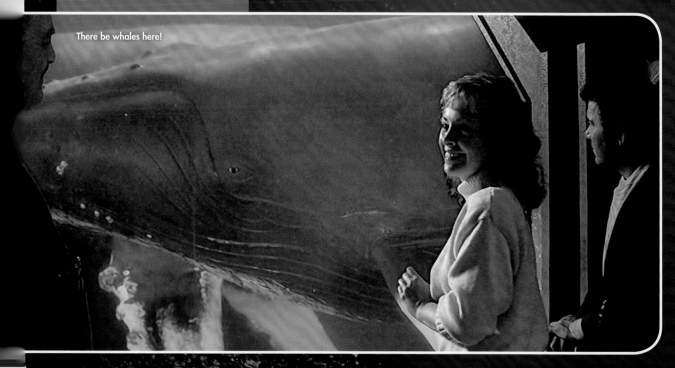

There be whales here!

Gillian seems right at home in the 23rd Century

Catherine Hicks

WHICH WITCH?

and [the parking lot] is full of water," she continues. "And there are these towers with these old studio men on top of them. One was in charge of the lightning. One was in charge of the rain. One was in charge of thunder. Then there was a big wave machine, too. And when Leonard called, 'Action,' you could feel old Hollywood just cranking up to create this storm. I couldn't believe it. I thought, 'This is so cool,' because I'd always wanted to do movies. Movies, to me, were what I wanted to do. I turned down all sorts of television. So I was so happy to finally be in a movie *and* to be in the parking lot that I used to park in as a TV actress!"

LIFE AFTER HEAVEN

These days, Hicks is nearly three decades past *Star Trek* and more than 25 years beyond another of her most memorable credits, the horror film *Child's Play*. It's also been six-plus years since *7th Heaven* ended its landmark run. The show cast the actress as Annie Camden, wife of Reverend Eric Camden, and mother to their brood of seven children. Rev. Camden was, of course, played by Stephen Collins – Will Decker in *Star Trek: The Motion Picture*.

In the years since *7th Heaven* entered its syndication afterlife, Hicks has stayed extremely active on both professional

and personal fronts. "I've done about 20 independent films and three plays," she says, but her focus has shifted, "I was gone a lot during *7th Heaven*, and I have enormous working-mom guilt because [my daughter] was overlooked, so, since she was placed near me for school, I'm here, I'm home. She calls, I'm home. So I've not been auditioning. I've been taking a year off to be home whenever she calls, and that feels totally right."

Looking back at *The Voyage Home*, Hicks ultimately loved the finished movie, but some mildly negative comments she made about *Star Trek* at the time, during a wide-ranging interview with *People Magazine*, were played up. "[It was] horrible," she says of the fallout of that interview, and the hurt it caused director Nimoy. "I confess that I was still ignorant [about *Star Trek*] until I saw [the movie]. I knew it was great when I saw it with my mom at the premiere, and I've come to love – love! – *Star Trek*, and be so grateful for how lucky I was.

"I'm just so proud of *The Voyage Home*, and when it airs on movie channels, I'm just tickled pink," Hicks reflects, "Everybody saw that film. It wasn't just a science fiction sideline, it was pretty mainstream, so it was a blessing at the time. I knew it was a great role. I knew they were great people. I didn't know that I was part of a certain history." ◢

Before her *Voyage Home*, Hicks played a crime-busting witch in the short-lived but wonderful series *Tucker's Witch*. "That was a fun show," says Hicks, "*Tucker's Witch* was something I did right after I had played Marilyn Monroe (in ABC's *Marilyn – The Untold Story*, for which Hicks scored an Emmy nomination). I wanted to do movies, but there had been a big actors' strike, so things had been quiet. That series came along at the right time."

"Tim Matheson and I played a romantic married couple who solved crimes together – he was a detective and I was a witch. I wanted to dress her like a punk, but they didn't go for it. It was a fun show, the first time I was lead in a series. Fun, fashionable, and I made money, so I enjoyed myself. I still wanted to make movies, so I was glad when it didn't go on."

Hicks replaced another future *Trek* star in the role – Kim Cattrall (who would later play Valeris in *The Undiscovered Country*). "Yes, that was so weird, because Kim and I crossed over like that several times. I originated the role in the play *Tribute* on Broadway, and she played it in the film with Jack Lemmon. Then I played her role on *Tucker!*"

Pat Jankiewicz

BON VOYAGE

Ken Ralston's name is legend within the visual effects community, having lent his talents to many of the most famous and ground-breaking effects movies ever made – including three of the most fondly remembered *Star Trek* films. The visual effects supremo talks Khan, creativity, and Klingon monster dogs... By Calum Wadell

Visual effects wizard Ken Ralston has been working at the top of his trade for over three decades, winning five Academy Awards in the process (including Oscars for 1985's fantasy-fable *Cocoon*, and 1994's *Forrest Gump*). He got his start on a certain 1977 movie called *Star Wars*, alongside now equally famous colleagues John Dykstra and Dennis Muren. Given that, post-*Star Wars*, the artist's CV would boast such blockbusters as *Back to the Future* (1985), *Who Framed Roger Rabbit* (1988), *The Mask* (1994), and *Men in Black II* (2002), it is perhaps little surprise that Ralston finds himself as one of Hollywood's most trusted, and celebrated, effects workers, and is currently chief Visual Effects Supervisor and Creative Head at Sony Pictures' Imageworks. However, speaking all these years later, the artist admits that some of his finest moments came on the set of *Star Trek*.

Playing a major part in the look and design of 1982's *The Wrath of Khan* (on which he is credited as the Special Visual Effects Supervisor), Ralston remained onboard for

The Search for Spock and concluded his duties with 1986's *The Voyage Home*.

"I was a huge fan, growing up, of *Star Trek*," he explains, "but I was disappointed by *The Motion Picture*. I saw it at the cinema and, to me, it just did not have the same feel that the TV series had. I think they tried to make it more of a sci-fi epic, but *Star Trek* was not *2001*. It was never intending to be Kubrick; it was its own thing – and when I came onboard for *The Wrath of Khan*, I know that was the feeling behind-the-scenes. The idea was to return to the feel of that great show that we all grew up watching."

Having worked on *Star Wars* and *The Empire Strikes Back* just prior to getting hired for *The Wrath of Khan*, Ralston admits that he could not believe his luck when another major sci-fi project came his way.

"I thought 'This is great, it is one brilliant movie after the next'", he says. "I cannot say exactly how *The Wrath of Khan* came to me, but I have some memories of speaking to the people at Paramount before I was hired. I remember that they wanted to keep *Star Trek* going, but they had not been entirely satisfied with that

first film either. I think the experience of making it had been difficult, and when it came out it had not done as well as they anticipated. Perhaps they were expecting profits like *Star Wars*, but I don't know – obviously there had been some comparison between that and *The Motion Picture* by the critics. I met the director of *The Wrath of Khan*, Nicholas Meyer, and the producers, and I hit it off with everyone. They could tell I was a fan of the series, and they hired me quite quickly. From there I was shipped off to the *Enterprise*, and away we went."

HARD AND FAST

Ralston also admits that it was surreal to find himself in the company of actors that had shaped some of his childhood interest in sci-fi and fantasy.

"Yeah, it was hilarious when I first met them all," he laughs. "It was actually a very weird experience to walk on the set of *The Wrath of Khan*, and see all of those guys sitting together. I introduced myself, of course, and kept thinking, 'Wow, I grew up watching

"EVERY ONE OF THE CAST AND CREW KNEW THAT WE WERE WORKING HARD TO MAKE SOMETHING SPECIAL."

these actors on the television.' It was good to get to know them a little bit. They were a pretty quirky bunch, but they got along with each other, and I was never made to feel like a stranger or anything."

The artist also reveals that *The Wrath of Khan* was a demanding but rewarding shoot.

"On that film I had a lot of people working with me," he mentions. "I had model guys who would jump through hoops for everything that I needed, and I had a bunch of people helping me with the lighting as well. I was doing a lot of tests for the visual effects during the production of that film, because we were really trying to break some new ground, which I think we did. So on a lot of the set-ups, I needed a good, fast team of helpers: there really was not a lot of time to mess around on *The Wrath of Khan*. It was a big production, that was designed to re-launch this franchise on the cinema screen. There was a lot depending on it. I was shooting almost everything myself, if I could. Where that wasn't possible, just because of the logistics of the effects work, I had a group of really able workers helping me out."

Despite commanding a team of highly efficient effects artists, Ralston admits that the production of *The Wrath of Khan* still demanded long and unsociable hours.

"We shot a lot of that movie at night," he continues. "I remember staying up late quite a few times, with a coffee in my hand, getting stuff done. Then I would go into the optical department in the morning and check on the shots, to see how they were looking. I would also pay close attention to the dailies. The director on *The Wrath of Khan*, Nicholas Meyer, is a very good filmmaker, and he really encouraged me to push things, and to come up with new ideas. I remember that he praised how the ships were looking against the blue screen, and the fluidity of their movement. Meanwhile, I was concerned about the lighting of the models we were making – they had to be lit in a certain way to look realistic. This was before CGI. If you didn't get everything right, then the audience would know that it was miniatures flying around in front of them. So I was in and out of several different department during the day, and everyone was trying to do

what I was explaining (*laughs*). It was a very challenging movie, but I think the end result speaks for itself. It remains a classic."

EEL APPEAL

Ralston also got the freedom to shoot one particularly macabre moment himself: namely, the unforgettably icky instance in which the titular tormentor (played by Ricardo Montalban) inserts Ceti eels into the helmets of Commander Pavel Chekov and Captain Clark Terrell. The creepy critters embed themselves into the brains of both explorers by crawling into their ears, in a nightmarish sequence that edged this initial *Star Trek* sequel into horror movie territory.

"I was left to shoot a lot of the Ceti eel sequence by myself," explains Ralston. "Nicholas really trusted me with that. From what I have heard, it is one of these moments where a lot of the audience looks away (*laughs*). I guess that attests to its power. I spent a little while sketching these eels, and then sculpting some three-dimensional

models. A lot of thought went into making them as horrible as they were (*laughs*). I remember that when we were doing that scene, everyone was very accommodating and was willing to do whatever it took to make it effective. We all knew that it was going to be an important moment in the movie, because it shows you how malicious and evil Khan is. I can still remember sticking the Ceti eel on Chekov's face and the actor, Walter Koenig, was brilliant to work with. He did not have a single complaint about this thing being glued to him."

Being in charge of the visual effects meant that Ralston became a trusted part of *The Wrath of Khan* and, consequently, had some additional opportunities to cast an influence on the making of the movie.

"Nicholas trusted me with some other stuff too," adds Ralston. "For instance, once we had completed the main stuff with the live-action crew, I would get to shoot a lot of the inserts. He was very open to ideas and collaboration, as long

as everything was looking good. Of course, I need to add that my team and I worked with his story-boards. It was not as if I ever said, 'Hey, today I am just going to just make a bunch of stuff from the top of my head.' The movie had to stay close to what the director wanted, but I really valued being allowed to do some of my own work on it."

GO COMPARE

Released to widespread audience acclaim, *The Wrath of Khan* remains a fan favorite, more than 30 years later. Indeed, those who despaired of the comparatively languorous pace of *The Motion Picture* had their wishes for a full-throttle sci-fi action thriller fulfilled by this second instalment.

"Every one of the cast and crew knew that we were working hard to make something special with *The Wrath of Khan*," affirms

Ralston. "I always pick that movie out as the *Star Trek* I had the most fun on. So, unsurprisingly, we went right into *The Search for Spock*. The good news for us was that *The Wrath of Khan* had been a big hit, so there was more money for the visual effects!"

Despite not being received on its release quite as favourably as *The Wrath of Khan*, the time may have come to reappraise *The Search for Spock*, directed by Leonard Nimoy, as a classic in its own right, certainly from an effects perspective. Featuring some of the finest back-drops and matte work in the original film series, as well as Christopher Lloyd in the role of Kruge – perhaps the most fearsome Klingon ever to threaten death and destruction on Kirk and crew – this second sequel more than holds its own. In addition, the visual effects are better than ever, with an entire planet (the crumbling and ready-to-explode *Genesis*) depicted in exotic and lavish detail. Also worth mentioning is the explosive fate of the *Enterprise* itself – arguably one of the most unforgettable moments in *Star Trek* lore.

"I don't know," ponders Ralston when asked to compare *The Search for Spock* with *The Wrath of Khan*. "I think that the whole tone and intention of *The Search for Spock* was different from the previous movie. *The Wrath of Khan*, for good or for bad – and most of us would say the former – captured that feel of the old show. *The Search for Spock* built on that, but it was really its own movie – and a very good one. I can't honestly say I like comparing them because they are actually very different." Ralston is also quick to enthuse about at least one creation from *The Search for Spock*.

"I think my favorite creation from that film is actually the monster dog

"I was shooting almost everything myself," says Ralston·

FROM CELLS TO CELLULOID

A sked about his own creative process, Ralston discloses that it all begins with a pad of paper and a pen. "Everything starts from a sketch, with me," he declares. "Even if my sketches are somewhat less than I want them to be, that whole process of drawing just puts my brain into a place where I can begin looking for basic forms. I have worked like that my entire life, and some of my best stuff has been done that way. I start to doodle and draw, and if something clicks, I will try and explore that in a drawing. Of course, I can only do that up to a certain point so, rather than show the director a bunch of sketches, I tend to assemble a model after that initial design period. Once you have a model, it gives someone a much better idea of what you want to do – and it also makes your own ideas a lot easier to sell to the person in charge (*laughs*)."

from the Klingon ship," he chuckles. "I remember showing Leonard [Nimoy] a handful of drawings for that, and he liked what I had done. It was the same with the *Bird-of-Prey*, which I really enjoyed creating. I liked working with Leonard. He was a very assertive director, and he knew that he wanted *The Search for Spock* to create its own atmosphere, so that it would not just be a retread of *The Wrath of Khan*."

HOME AND DRY

Of course, when it came to Ralston's final stint on the *Enterprise*, with 1986's *The Voyage Home*, things changed again. This time, the tone of the film was more light-hearted, abandoning a lot of the malevolence and mystery that had driven the story to *The Search for Spock*. Once again, though, it was Leonard Nimoy calling the shots from behind the camera.

"It was good to work with Leonard when we did the fourth film," says Ralston. "I recall that when I did *The Voyage Home*, I said to myself, 'I should really try and meet Gene Roddenberry,' but that never happened. I did three *Star Trek* movies and never got to shake the hand of the guy who created the series, which is quite strange. It was fun to return to that world, although I recall that *The Voyage Home* was done on a slightly tighter schedule than the other two films. It was a movie that required a great deal of creativity. We shot it in San Francisco, and it was quite compressed insofar as what we had to do, and what time we had to do it in."

Now, of course, much of *Star Trek*'s future world is created with the assistance of CGI.

Ralston, as an innovator of the form, is pleased to see these technical advances, but admits he misses the 'good old days' of practical visual effects work.

"If CGI is in the hands of the right people, and used the right way, then it is wonderful," he states. "But I think today, at the cinema, you see a lot of stuff that relies on it too much. The big problem is that any kind of computer graphic is very difficult to composite and light, not to mention getting it to the point where it looks real. That can become a nightmare, although the technology is getting better and better. On the other hand, though, what you get with CGI is security. You can spend weeks building something and it just breaks when the director calls 'action'. So I see the benefits of doing these things, even the simplest of objects, with a computer." Ralston also believes audiences find practical effects easier to connect with. "In general, I think it is very difficult to take an audience to a place where they stop looking at what is on-screen as an effect," he explains, "but when you build a model, or you have a real creature on the set, you get that suspension of disbelief, because it is obviously, actually there. For me, personally, I am happy to use CGI, but I think it should always come down to what is best for the film."

"I am still a fan," Ralston reveals, when asked if he would consider another stint in the *Star Trek* universe, should the opportunity ever afford itself, "As long as there is a chance to be creative, I'm always interested in returning to the drawing board!" ⋀

OTHER GREAT TV TIE-IN COMPANIONS FROM TITAN
ON SALE NOW!

**The X-Files - The Bureau
and The Syndicate**
ISBN 9781782763710

**The X-Files - Monsters
and Villains**
ISBN 9781782763727

**The X-Files - The Truth,
Secrets & Lies**
ISBN 9781782763734

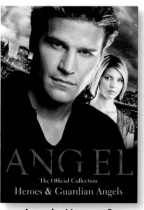

**Angel - Heroes &
Guardian Angels**
ISBN 9781782763680

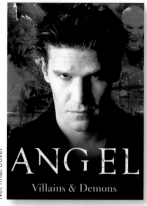

Not final Cover

**Angel - Villains
& Demons**
ISBN 9781782763697

**Star Wars - The Official
Collection Volume 1**
ISBN 9781785851162

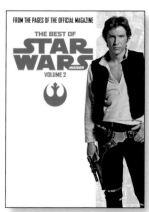

**Star Wars - The Official
Collection Volume 2**
ISBN 9781785851179

COMING SOON

**Buffy - Welcome to
the Hellmouth**
ISBN 9781782763642

**Buffy -
Fear, Itself**
ISBN 9781782763659

**Buffy - Magic &
Witchcraft**
ISBN 9781782763666

**Once Upon a Time-
Behind the Magic**
ISBN 9781782760290

For more information visit www.titan-comics.com
STAR TREK MAGAZINE SUBSCRIPTIONS: TITANMAGAZINES.COM/TREK

TITANCOMICS